THE SAMPLER

Patterns for Composition

THE SAMPLER

Patterns for Composition

Rance G. Baker
San Antonio College

Billie R. Phillips
San Antonio College

D.C. HEATH AND COMPANY
Lexington, Massachusetts   Toronto

Copyright © 1979 by D.C. Heath and Company.

All rights reserved. No part of this publication may be reproduced or transmitted in any form or by any means, electronic or mechanical, including photocopy, recording, or any information storage or retrieval system, without permission in writing from the publisher.

Published simultaneously in Canada.

Printed in the United States of America.

International Standard Book Number: 0-669-02267-5

Library of Congress Catalog Card Number: 79-83693

Preface

Designed for beginning composition students in college, *The Sampler: Patterns for Composition* is based on the five-hundred-word theme or essay. It consists of introductory explanations and definitions, examples of paragraphs and essays written by students, and suggested brief assignments that encourage students to write their own thesis statements, topic sentences, transitional devices, and outlines.

The Sampler is organized around two units, the paragraph and the essay. Part I, "The Paragraph," provides brief explanations and definitions of the rhetorical methods of developing and organizing paragraphs. Each explanation is followed by several samples of writing illustrating that particular rhetorical method. Part I gives students a basis for organizing and developing the longer expository and persuasive essays also required in most composition courses.

Part II, "The Essay," explains and illustrates the planning and writing of expository essays. Most of the essays were written by college students and exemplify the basic form of the five-hundred-word essay: a title, an introductory paragraph (which presents the thesis statement), developmental paragraphs (which support or argue the parts of the thesis sentence), and a final summary paragraph. The essays reflect good student writing, but are not meant to exemplify polished, professional models.

This book can supplement both composition readers, which consist mainly of professional essays, and rhetoric-handbook texts, which some students need to help them identify and resolve mechanical problems. The models of writing included will help students more easily understand the expository methods that they should use.

We wish to thank all of those who helped us obtain sample paragraphs and essays, especially the students who labored in composition classes at San Antonio College and then gave us permission to share their writing with other students. In addition, we wish to thank Lawrence Bell, Chairman of the Government Department at Tarrant

County Junior College, Northeast Campus, Fort Worth, Texas, and Bob Polunsky, film critic for *The San Antonio Light* newspaper and television station KENS in San Antonio, for allowing publication of samples of their writing. Finally, we acknowledge the helpful criticism provided by Professors Jack Klug and John Ullmer of San Antonio College as *The Sampler* grew from mimeographed pages into a textbook.

We feel that the explanations and samples of writing in this text will help students in composition courses become more confident writers.

R.G.B.
B.R.P.

Contents

PART 1

The Paragraph

History and Definition   2

SECTION 1 **Characteristics of the Well-Written Paragraph**   5
     Unity   5
     Order   7
     Coherence   12
     Completeness   18
     Appropriate Style   20
     Paragraph Checklist   21

SECTION 2 **Methods of Paragraph Development**   23
     Development by Example   23
     Development by Contrast   27
     Development by Comparison   31
     Development by Analogy   36
     Development by Statistics   39
     Development by Definition   43

SECTION 3 **Paragraph Development Through Analysis**   49
     Analysis by Structure   49
     Analysis by Function   53
     Analysis by Process   55

        Analysis by Classification 58
        Analysis by Cause/Effect 61

SECTION 4 Descriptive and Narrative Paragraphs   67
        Description 67
        Narrative 72

PART II
The Essay

Definition and History   84

SECTION 1 Mechanics of the Essay   87
        Thesis Sentence 87
        Outline 92
        Introductory Paragraph 99
        Summary Paragraph 103

SECTION 2 The Expository Essay   109
        Exposition by Enumeration 109
        Exposition by Contrast 115
        Exposition by Comparison 123
        Exposition by Definition 127

SECTION 3 The Analytical Essay   135
        Analysis by Structure 135
        Analysis by Function 141
        Analysis by Process 146
        Analysis by Classification 152
        Analysis by Cause/Effect 160

SECTION 4 The Persuasive Essay   167
        Logical Argument 167
        Illogical Argument 174

THE SAMPLER
Patterns for Composition

PART I

The Paragraph

History and Definition of the Paragraph

Before paragraphs were indented, a typeset page looked like this:

XXXXXXXXXXXXXXX
XXXXXXXXXXXXXXX
XXXXXXXXXXXXXXX
XXXXXXXXXXXXXXX

However, a solid page of unbroken type was difficult to read. When manuscripts were handwritten, the page was broken up by small pictures (illuminations) and various sizes and styles of calligraphy. With printed material, however, such variations were not as easy or as possible. Consequently, printers took matters into their own hands and began to decorate the printed page with various signs and symbols. Some of these (# & *) are still found on the top row of keys on a typewriter. One of the symbols, the *pilkrow* (¶), was placed in the margin or scattered throughout the printed page to break up the solid block of type. The page might look like this:

XXXXXXXXX¶XXXXXXXXX
XXXXX¶XXXXXXX¶XXXXX
XX¶XXXXXXXXXXXXX¶XX
¶XXXXXXXXXXXXXXXXX¶
XXX¶XXXXXXXXXXX¶XXX
XXXXXXX¶XXXX¶XXXXXX

Another way to break up the page was to indent some line on a page several spaces in from the left- or right-hand margin. Through a rather involved series of circumstances, the pilkrow became the sign or symbol the printer used to indicate indention; it was thus the forefather of the present-day paragraph.

Indention, then, started as a printing practice, but writers later began to use it as a method of introducing a new subject. After all, they saw it in print, so the practice had to be good for something. It took American rhetoricians, however, until near the end of the nineteenth century to develop the idea of the **topic sentence**. The development of that idea turned the paragraph into a genuine and identifiable writing unit. The word *paragraph* (which once meant "to write in the margin") now means to indent from the left margin (or, if using block-style paragraphing, to leave a blank line). Americans have added a variety of adjectives to the word to designate functional units of composition. Some of these are *introductory, developmental, transitional, dialogue, concluding,* and *narrative*. Thus, the paragraph is now a unit of composition that serves a variety of functions.

The introductory paragraph is a statement of about 75–100 words. Its purpose is to present the thesis of the composition, thus acquainting the reader with not only the topic but also the control of the topic.

The **transitional paragraph** is usually much shorter than other paragraphs. Its purpose is to lead the reader from one major topic to another. In most five-hundred-word essays, a transitional paragraph is not needed. Normally, transitional words and phrases, or just one sentence, will suffice for the transition.

The **developmental paragraph** is usually about 100–150 words, depending upon the complexity of the central idea that is being developed. Also, the developmental paragraph may be a single unit complete within itself, or it may be part of a larger composition such as an essay, a dissertation, or a book.

The **summary paragraph**, sometimes called the concluding paragraph, is simply a restatement of what the essay discussed. Many times, the summary in a five-hundred-word essay is merely one or more sentences that restate the thesis sentence.

A paragraph should be indented five to seven spaces (be consistent), and looks like this on a page:

XXXX X XXX XXX. X XXXX XXXX XXX XXX XXXXX XX XXXX XXXX; XXX XX XXXXX XX XXXX XX XXXX XXXXX XXXXX XXX XX XXXX. XX XXX, XX XXX XXXXXXX XXX XX XXXX XXXX X XX XXXXXXXX XXXX XXXXX XXXX XXX XXXXXXXX XXX XXX XXXXXXXXX. XX XXX XXXX XX XXXXXXXX XXXX XXXX XXXX XXXXX XXXXXX XXXXXX.

SECTION 1

Characteristics of the Well-Written Paragraph

In addition to providing information, you must observe four characteristics or qualities in composing a paragraph. These characteristics are **unity**, **order**, **coherence**, and **completeness**.

Unity in the Paragraph

To understand paragraph unity, you must first be aware of the function of a topic sentence. Most paragraphs consist of two parts: the topic sentence and the developing sentences. The **topic sentence**, which is the most general statement in the paragraph, contains both the topic being discussed and the controlling idea about that topic. For example, a topic sentence such as "Without a doubt, Felix is rude" contains a subject (Felix) and the controlling idea that will be discussed about Felix (rudeness).

The **developing sentences** of the paragraph will then give support to the controlling idea by fully discussing the concept of rudeness in relation to Felix. The paragraph, in order to be unified, will *not* discuss that Felix goes to church, that he is handsome or ugly, that he has bad health, or that he is a brilliant student. The supporting sentences *will* illustrate the rudeness of Felix.

In the following topic sentences, pick out the subject and the controlling idea:

1. For the average college freshman, registration is the most frustrating aspect of the first semester.

2. Despite his being one of the greatest presidents of the United States, Abraham Lincoln had three major political weaknesses.
3. Serving in the Peace Corps is a rewarding experience.
4. Winters in Dillon, Montana, are miserable.
5. "A stitch in time saves nine" is impossible to live up to.

Remember, for a paragraph to be unified, each supporting sentence must relate to and develop the controlling idea in the topic sentence. With this in mind, analyze the first paragraph following. First, determine the subject and controlling idea in the topic sentence. Second, read the supporting sentences and decide which statements are relevant to and support the controlling idea. Third, decide which statements are irrelevant to the controlling idea and therefore should not be in the paragraph.

Once you have analyzed the first paragraph, read carefully the second paragraph. Then, using the same procedure you used in analyzing the first paragraph, determine whether this paragraph is unified.

● *Sample Paragraphs*

Biloxi, Mississippi

Biloxi, Mississippi, is basically an industrial city. It is one of the largest shrimp and oyster shipping points in the country. Biloxi is located on the Gulf of Mexico about eighty miles northeast of New Orleans. In 1699, it was settled by the French, and it was the capital of the Louisiana Territory until 1722. Some of the most interesting sites in Biloxi are Beauvoir, the home of Jefferson Davis, and the lighthouse, which was built in 1848. Located about twelve miles south of the city is Ship Island, which was the harbor for French exploration and settlement from 1699 to 1720. Ship Island is most notable as the landing place for the first marriageable girls for early French colonists. During World War II, Biloxi's population increased because Keesler Field, a military airport, was within the city limits. A veterans' home and a United States Coast Guard air station are two other federal installations in Biloxi. Also, the Louisville & Nashville Railroad furnishes transportation for the local industries. The year-round mild climate, along with its location on the Gulf, makes Biloxi a popular tourist center and resort. Boatbuilding and seafood packing are the predominant local industries.

Linda Hollowell

Importation of Minerals and Metals

According to the United States Department of the Interior, the United States import reliance upon select minerals and metals for consumption in 1977 heavily depended upon many countries outside of the Western Hemisphere. For example, Asiatic and Mediterrean countries made up a one-to-one ratio of importation of minerals and metals compared to that of other countries. These imports included 30% of the heavier metals such as columbium, mica, and tin, along with 20% of the softer minerals such as gypsum, vanadium, and sulphur. Surprisingly, communist countries were heavy exporters of many metals, especially in fields necessary for defensive purposes. These countries provided the United States with 76.3% of such metals as cobalt, platinum, chromium, and gold. The Western Hemisphere of Canada, Mexico, and South America did, however, have an open and continuous flow of metals and minerals into the United States. These countries made up a 12% production intake by the United States with their metals of mica, asbestos, zinc, and iron ore. The communist countries have a 38% production for consumption here, and the Asiatic and Mediterranean countries share the remaining 50% of the importation of minerals and metals relied on by the United States.

Richard Smith

Order in the Paragraph

>The order of development a paragraph follows depends sometimes on the subject matter and sometimes on the writer's purpose or preference. Most narrative and descriptive writing has a natural organization.

The narrative paragraph almost always follows chronological, or time, order. The writer starts with the first point and its time and continues to the last point and its time. The narrative may, however, be ordered by importance; the writer begins with the least important event and moves toward the most important event. The descriptive paragraph will follow the orderly movement through space, such as left to right, here to there, clockwise, or east to north to west to south. Thus, narrative and descriptive writing will follow the natural order of time and space, and sometimes of importance.

There are times, however, when you as a writer must apply an arbitrary order to the paragraphs, especially when the writing is expository. Three common kinds of order are explained and illustrated in the following pages: general-to-specific, specific-to-general, and question-to-answer.

GENERAL-TO-SPECIFIC ORDER

General-to-specific order (sometimes called "deductive order") is the most common kind of organization for an expository paragraph. The first sentence is the topic sentence and presents the general idea that will be developed. All other sentences in the paragraph specifically explain and support the generalization made in the topic sentence. The specific material may be handled by using statistics, examples, comparisons, or any other form of paragraph development. The following paragraph is an example of general-to-specific order.

● *Sample Paragraph*

The Police Officer

A police officer must observe many details in the process of investigating the scene of a crime. He must first, upon arriving at the scene, determine that a crime has been committed. After he has determined this, he must then determine what type of crime happened. The next detail that the officer must follow is to protect the crime scene. This is done so that any evidence present will not be destroyed. Next, the officer must ask any people around if they witnessed the crime. If there are any witnesses, the officer will either take their names and addresses or ask them to wait and talk with other investigators who may arrive. If the crime is a murder, the officer will search the surrounding area for the murder weapon. After the search, he will then patrol the area to see if he can find and arrest a suspect. After the investigation of the crime scene is completed, the officer must file a report on the crime.

Charles Caknupp

SPECIFIC-TO-GENERAL ORDER

Specific-to-general order (sometimes called "inductive order") is exactly the opposite of that explained above. It begins with specific statements and ends with a general summary or conclusion. This last sentence serves as a topic sentence. Again, any or a combination of the kinds of paragraph development may be used to lead to the topic sentence. The following paragraphs are examples of specific-to-general order.

● *Sample Paragraphs*

The Buffalo

To the Plains Indians, the buffalo was the principal means of life. The buffalo skin was used to make clothing and shelter. The bones were used to make tools, weapons, and ornaments. The meat was used as the main staple of the Indian's diet, and much of it was "jerked" and stored for long droughts and cold winters. Then came the frontiersmen and the buffalo hunters from east of the Mississippi River. These new hunters began to kill off the great buffalo herds by the thousands. The Plains Indians were forced to move continuously in search of new herds. However, within a matter of a few years, the once-great herds had dwindled down to a few individual buffalo. The Indians, who by this time were tired of starving and fighting, had to completely surrender their old way of life to the newer, white man's way. Thus, as a result of the white man's killing off the buffalo, the Plains Indians died, too.

Dan Taylor

The War of Jenkins' Ear

　　A war broke out between England and Spain in October of 1739. Relations between the two countries had been strained since the Peace of Utrecht in 1713, but war had been averted mainly through the efforts of British Prime Minister Robert Walpole. However, in 1731, a Scottish merchant ship, the <u>Rebecca</u>, was stopped and searched by a Spanish galleon. The <u>Rebecca</u>'s captain, Robert Jenkins, accused the Spanish of cutting off his ear. Jenkins approached various authorities about his maltreatment, but his complaint fell on deaf ears. So, seven years later, Jenkins wrote directly to King George II and included a severed ear in his report. The ear so ired the House of Commons that within a year England declared war on Spain. Most of the fighting was at first in South America, but eventually the hostilities developed into a major European war which lasted until 1748. After the war, the full truth finally came out. Jenkins' ear, which he claimed had been lost in service to England, had actually been cut off by Scottish authorities to punish Jenkins for fraud and thievery. Wars, both large and small, have started for various reasons, but perhaps the strangest reason on record is that which began the War of Jenkins' Ear.

　　　　　　　　　　　　　　　　　　　　C. B. Handle

QUESTION-TO-ANSWER ORDER
Question-to-answer order has a question serve as the topic sentence. The question presents the topic and the controlling idea, and the rest of the paragraph specifically answers the question posed in the topic sentence. Question-to-answer order follows principally the order of general to specific. The paragraph is developed by using examples, comparisons, and such. The following paragraph is an example of question-to-answer order.

● *Sample Paragraph*

Procrastination

Just how can you, a new college student, successfully carry out the ancient art of procrastination and thus carry on that noble tradition of not handing in assignments on time? The first and probably most effective means of procrastination in relation to writing an assignment is the inability to decide on a decent topic. Frequently this occurs when you are faced with a deadline, but you put off all thoughts of the dreaded assignment until the night before it is due. This leads to the next step: never do the assignment the day that it is assigned. Wait until tomorrow, or the weekend, when you will have plenty of time to write. Another point related to the previous one is never put the assignment higher on the totem pole of activities than, say, cleaning out the garage or changing the oil in your car. In other words, if there is something else to do besides writing, do it! It is infinitely more desirable to "play now, write later" than to do the opposite. Also, never be misled by those radicals who insist on doing assignments far before the deadline; it is they who will try to pressure you into the sinful temptation (Heaven forbid!) of being ready ahead of time with a completed assignment. So, in closing this easy "how to" lesson on procrastination, the main point can be summed up: "I'll do it later." If you use this as a guideline for later efforts not to do assignments, you can be assured of the satisfaction of sweating it out while the irresponsible student seated next to you glumly ponders the task of handing his paper in on time--a fate fit for neither man, nor beast, nor typical college student.

                                                    Douglas Walton

Coherence in the Paragraph

Coherence in a paragraph is the device of making words, phrases, and sentences flow smoothly and logically from one to the other. In other words, the ideas are so interwoven and "glued" together that the reader will be able to see the consistent relationship between them.

It is obvious that if a paragraph is not unified, does not have a logical order, and does not have a consistent point of view, then the reader is unlikely to grasp the point of the paragraph. So, granted that the paragraph does have unity, a logical order, and a consistent point of view, there are still other devices and techniques that you as a writer must be aware of in order to achieve coherence.

In general, the coherence devices most helpful for making your communication clear and for the reader in understanding your writing are transitional words and phrases, repetition of key words and phrases, pronoun reference, and parallel sentence structure.

TRANSITIONAL WORDS AND PHRASES

One of the most common methods of establishing coherence in a paragraph is using transitional words and phrases. These devices indicate to the reader the specific relationshp between what was said and what will be said.

Within a sentence, the coordinate conjunctions provide a coherent link to indicate relationships between parallel elements. The word *and* indicates a comparable idea; *but* and *yet* indicate a contrasting idea; *or* and *nor* indicate an alternative idea; *for* indicates a reason for a result already stated; and *so* indicates a conclusion from reasons already stated.

Also within a sentence, correlative conjunctions are used to establish relationships between parallel elements. The conjunctions *either/or*, *neither/nor*, and *whether/or (not)* are used to indicate parallel alternatives. The conjunctions *not only/but (also)* and *both/and* indicate parallel similarities.

Just as coordinate and correlative conjunctions show specific relationships between elements in a sentence, so there are words and phrases that mark specific relationships between the sentences themselves. The following is a list of categories and words that signify transitional relationships:

> To signify an **additional idea:** *also, moreover, again, further, furthermore, in addition, likewise, too, first, initially, second, third, next, finally, last, another, other, then*
>
> To signify a **comparison:** *likewise, similarly, in a like manner, in comparison, so it is.*

Coherence in the Paragraph

To signify a **contrast**... ...theless, still, unlike, in contrast, conversely, on ... the other hand, whereas

To signify a **cause-effect**... ...herefore, thus, hence, then, consequently, according... ...n, as a result

To signify an **example** or ...ing: for example, for instance, to illustrate, for ...quently, in general, in particular, namely, usually, ...

To signify a **summary**: to sum... ...rize, in short, to conclude, in conclusion, on the wh...

The following paragraphs illustrat... ...rough the use of transitional words and phrases. As you ... ...raphs, determine what words, phrases, and coordinate c... ...onjunctions are used. Then determine the specific rela... ...how between the words or phrases they link in a coherer...

● **Sample Paragraphs**

The Lost A

A funny thing happened to me on the way to E... ...ass. As I went into registration last August, I was prepared to sign up for the class I had been dreading most, freshman composition. I had done all my research properly and had found that the general consensus was, "Take Loveless; if a person can't make an A in his class, he must be really stupid." As I approached the English section, a pretty, middle-aged lady asked, "May I help you?" I don't recall what it was about her that intimidated me, but she had me thinking that a life of motherhood would surpass English 601a. It couldn't have been the fact that when she checked my proof-of-eligibility she chuckled sarcastically and asked, "Are you sure you want to try again?" I failed to see the humor in the question, especially since I was not completely convinced that I did want to "try again." I tried to act intelligent by letting her know exactly what I wanted: "I want to register for composition with Professor Loveless." She smiled and said, "Well, you can't have that class; it's full." The next few minutes were spent debating and explaining. She said, "I know what you've heard!" I then tried the old trick of claiming, "I have to have English at that particular time or I can't take it." She promptly showed me that there were seven other freshman comp. classes available at that same time. I really felt like crying; my plans had been wrecked! As I stood before her like a mute, she leaned over, looked me in the eye, and said, "Take Professor Pliant; I think he's what you're looking for." A "Grizzly Adams" type man next to her smiled and agreed: "You'll like him. He's a good ole' boy, a kicker, a graduate of Sul Ross, and forty years ole'." I failed to understand what those qualifications had to do with my ability to overcome a previous grade of D in English; however, the teacher looked as if he knew what he was talking about, so I accepted the computer card. Later, I found out that the lady who recommended Professor Pliant also taught the same class at the same time. Sure enough, "Grizzly Adams" was Professor Pliant, and I've been wondering ever since why Ms. Helpful didn't want me in her own class. Maybe she had a grudge against Pliant; maybe she had a grudge against me for wanting an easy A.

Becky Bolling

A Love-Hate Relationship

I generally love my cat, but at four o'clock in the morning, I literally despise her. No matter how late my cat has stayed out the night before, she is wide awake and ready for action at four o'clock. How do I know? First, I hear a low cry and then a loud crash. I now know that one of two things has occurred: either Wickenburg, Arizona, has had its first earthquake, or my cat has knocked over my fifty-pound desk. If by this time I haven't responded, phase two begins: my once-loved cat begins to climb my velveteen curtains. Once at the top, she carefully measures the distance between my bed and herself and leaps gracefully onto my prone form. It has now become a battle of nerves. How far will she go before I either go crazy or give in and throw the destructive monster out of my second floor window? My cat next sharpens her claws on my bed post, leaving tidy little scars on my used-to-be-good furniture. Finally, to show how well she has honed them, she demonstrates their cutting ability by playing with my unprotected arm or hand. By this time, I give in and take her outside. When I get back upstairs and into my bed, the alarm rings and it is again time for me to prepare to face the world. After two and one-half hours of fighting to escape the house, why does my cat sit at the back door and scratch the screen until she can come in and take a nap?

Jean Dalglish

REPETITION OF KEY WORDS AND PHRASES

Although careless and needless repetition creates awkwardness and sometimes incoherence within a sentence or paragraph, a careful repetition of key words and ideas, often with slight variations, can transfer the thoughts smoothly throughout the paragraph unit. How can you as a writer differentiate between a key word and a secondary word? Normally, the key word or words will center around the subject and controlling idea of the topic sentence. Specifically, the key words and phrases are those that are used throughout the paragraph, not just in a limited portion of it.

Also keep in mind that synonyms closely related to the key words are effective as a coherence device. Use synonyms when repeating key words becomes too awkward or monotonous.

The following paragraph illustrates coherence through the repetition of key words. As you read the paragraph, identify the key words and phrases that are repeated.

● *Sample Paragraph*

The UFO

A UFO is an instrument of travel which enables unknown life forms to traverse both time and space and come to where we are. The UFO is always in the form of some unimaginably fast and highly maneuverable airship, never seemingly suited for sea or ground. It appears out of nowhere, and for a moment some people see its round or cigar shape, its small windows, and its bright lights. Then, like fog in the early-morning sunshine, it vanishes, and, like the wind, leaves people to wonder from where it came. Sometimes a UFO is called a flying saucer or a saucer-shaped object, and it has been sighted and even photographed on many occasions in all parts of the world. But, so far, people know only what is literally implied by the name "UFO." The expression "UFO" began as an acronym for "unidentified flying object." However, most modern dictionaries have made UFO a full-fledged noun, complete with a pronunciation key and a plural form. It is strange how concreteness can sometimes be born out of nothingness.

Paul Hewitt

PRONOUN REFERENCE

Like the repetition of key words, pronoun reference is often used as a coherence device. Because most pronouns have a noun antecedent clearly established in a paragraph, they refer back and provide a link between sentences. Many times, pronouns are used in conjunction with key words, and they can be used to break monotonous repetition.

The following paragraph illustrates coherence achieved through the use of pronoun reference. As you read the paragraph, identify the pronouns and their antecedents. Also, look for key words that may be used.

● *Sample Paragraph*

Leo

My husband, Leo, is a perfect husband. His understanding and caring make him perfect. He is always near when I need him, and he is ready to help at anything. He is strong and gives me security. However, there are moments when he is gentle and makes me feel very much a woman. He works hard every day, and he brings home a check at the end of every week. He enjoys the simple things in life, like sports, music, and his family. Leo is ambitious, and he strives to succeed in his educational goal. He protects what is his and leaves alone what is not. Most of all, he loves me. Perfect he is. But he could never be perfect without the enormous capacity for understanding which he possesses.

Rita Ann Vasquez

PARALLEL SENTENCE STRUCTURE
Just as parallel coordinate structure is essential to understanding the meaning of a sentence, so can the use of parallel sentence structure within a paragraph help coherence. Parallel sentence structure works principally as a coherence device by helping the reader maintain the relationship between the developing sentences and the subject and controlling idea.

The following paragraph illustrates how the use of parallel sentence structure helps coherence. As you read the paragraph, determine how each sentence is parallel and is related to topic the sentence.

● *Sample Paragraph*

The Good Coach and The Bad Coach

A knowledge of his sport and a dedicated application of this knowledge mark the differences between a good coach and a bad coach. First, the good coach reads and studies different types of drills and plays which he will incorporate into his team's practices and competitions; the bad coach merely settles upon the few drills and plays that he has a knowledge of. The good coach is always prepared for practices and has a definite plan of what he wants from his players; the bad coach is unprepared and undecided not only about his intentions but also about what he expects from his team. Also, the good coach dedicates himself to his team and expects the same dedication from his players. He will not accept flimsy excuses for missing practice, and he will not tolerate a player's giving less than one hundred per cent. However, the bad coach shows his lack of dependability and responsibility by being too easy with discipline. He accepts players' missing practice for almost any reason and his team's being passive instead of aggressive. The good coach is firm and lets his team know where he stands and what he expects; the bad coach practically allows his team to take control. Most often, the good coach's knowledge and ability will lead him and his team to a winning season; the bad coach will have to tolerate losing most of the games, and probably his job.

Lana Huennehens

Completeness in the Paragraph

Completeness in a paragraph means that the controlling idea is developed thoroughly by the use of particular (specific) information. Thus, completeness is relative to how complex or general the topic sentence is. For example, one paragraph can give a reader a sense of completeness in seventy-five words, while another paragraph might require two hundred words to accomplish the same effect.

The type of development (see Section 2, Methods of Paragraph Development) that the writer chooses will also dictate the so-called length or brevity required to explain an idea. For example, it will usually take a much longer paragraph to define fully the word *placebo* than it will to explain the process of taking a prescribed medication. To define fully the word *placebo* may require three hundred words; to fully explain the process of taking a pill may require only three to ten words.

Examine the following paragraphs for completeness. Notice that the first leaves the reader with a sense of incompleteness, if not bewilderment. The second paragraph more fully explains the idea, and it gives a sense of completeness.

● *Sample Paragraphs*

Bullfighting

For a number of years, I was intrigued by bullfighting. It began when I worked with a girl who always talked about it, and a few years later, a local television station showed bullfights on Saturday nights. Several years later, we were in Mexico and went to see a bullfight first hand. While we were in Mexico, we learned that the term <u>bullfighting</u> is frowned upon by those fans of the sport. The first two bullfighters couldn't make a kill. The next bullfighter was gored, but he killed his bull, anyway. The main event featured Charles Nixon, who, after three attempts, finally got his bull down; however, it got back up as we were leaving. Needless to say, I haven't been back to any more of these spectacles.

                         Bullfighting

   For a number of years I was intrigued by bullfighting. This fascination began when I worked with a girl who was an <u>aficionada</u>. She was always talking about bullfights and telling stories about different <u>toreros</u>. She even lent me several books on the subject. A few years later, a local television station offered Saturday-night programs of bullfights originating in Spain. The films were in beautiful color; the music was stirring, and the crowds were most enthusiastic. Several more years had passed when my husband and I found ourselves in Matamores, Mexico, one bright and sunny morning. We saw a poster advertising a bullfight, and off we went to see the spectacle. It began badly, with a band hopelessly off key; cowardly horses that had to be blind-folded and led into the arena; and bulls, behaving not like fire-breathing-ground pawers but like pussy-cats. First, two butchers who couldn't make a kill with their swords needed an attendant with a knife to dispatch their bulls. Although the next <u>torero</u> was gored, he managed to finish his bull with the sword. Finally, a pudgy McAllen native, Charles Nixon, dressed in a bright-aqua, stretch-elastic costume, entered the ring, bowed to the crowd, and turned his attention to the bull. As soon as he felt the time was right, he lunged and drove his sword into the bull's throat--and out the other side. The bull walked away. Since Mr. Nixon was unable to retrieve his own sword, several clowns distracted the bull while an attendant removed the sword. I was losing my interest in bullfights when Mr. Nixon once more took his sword and plunged it cleanly just behind the animal's head; the bull crumpled into a heap in the dust. Exalted, Mr. Nixon walked away, bowing and posturing to the crowd. We also began to walk away, but before we reached the stairs, we heard the unexpected sound of laughter. Turning around for one last look, I saw Mr. Nixon, still bowing and smiling, being glared at by the enraged bull, back on its feet. I don't know how that all ended because we left. I do know that this was my first, and very probably my last, bullfight.

Kathryn L. Adams

Appropriate Style in the Paragraph

There are several important items you should consider when choosing the style you will use in your writing. We will discuss two of them, point of view and sexism, here; see also Section 4, "Descriptive and Narrative Paragraphs," for a discussion of a third—whether to use a personal, subjective style or an impersonal, objective one.

CHOOSING POINT OF VIEW
You should always consider your audience, the people who will read what you write. If your paragraph or essay is written for a general, unlimited audience, you don't want to limit that audience by using the second-person personal pronoun *you* in an impersonal way. If you, as writer, are directing your remarks to a specific reader or readers (such as a friend or an employee of the Internal Revenue Service), use *you*. If, however, you are directing your information to a general reading audience, nouns and third-person pronouns will be more effective (*one, anyone, everyone, students, the person*).

When pronouns are used, many instructors require students to use the third-person forms in the belief that such use forces the writing to be objective (a desirable quality) and consistent. Use of the third person also precludes possible resentment on the reader's part. For example, a paper that is directed to a general audience and that discusses the merits of dieting might cause the reader who is not obese to resent the statements, "You are so fat that you have trouble entering your car. You should restrict your food intake." A more objective, and therefore acceptable, comment would allow the general reader to understand such a restriction for any obese person. Such a reader would not be offended if you wrote, "The obese person may find entering a car difficult. This overweight person should restrict his or her intake of food." Some instructors suggest the use of passive voice: "The intake of food should be restricted."

Both instructions and explanations in *The Sampler* use the second-person *you*, because this book has an audience composed of students who are being specifically and directly addressed. The samples themselves almost always use third-person pronouns to refer to the reader(s). For exceptions, see the section on Process Analysis, page 146.

AVOIDING SEXIST PRONOUNS
Because the English language does not contain a third-person, singular personal pronoun that refers to both masculine and feminine individuals, the aware writer who does not want to offend equality-conscious readers recognizes that a problem exists: "Everyone must bring __?__ books to class. Each worker should put in __?__ two cents' worth." Should the writer use the masculine, possessive pronoun *his* in the blanks and offend those readers who believe, rightly, that women *and* men should bring books to class and that both males *and* females work and should put in "two cents' worth"? Or should the writer, not wishing to offend either sex, choose the ungrammatical third-person, plural pronoun *their* to refer to the singular subjects *everyone* and *each worker*? Consider this sentence, for example: "After a writer chooses a subject, *she/he/they* go(es) to the library to research that subject."

The media are dealing with this problem in several as-yet nonstandard ways. One magazine uses *s/he* to convey both *she* and *he;* but *hir (him* or *her)* and *hes (hers* or *his)* may be confusing. Although the British are accepting the heretofore ungrammatical plural to refer to a singular subject (*their* instead of *he* or *she*), many instructors in the United States prefer the grammatically correct and traditionally accepted masculine-singular pronoun, in spite of the offense it causes many people. We can only advise you to ask your instructor what his or her preferences are.

PARAGRAPH CHECKLIST

A. Consult this page each time you finish a writing assignment involving one or more paragraphs.

1. Is the paragraph indented?
2. Does the paragraph have a clear topic sentence with a clear subject and a clear controlling idea?

22   Characteristics of the Well-Written Paragraph

3. Are all of the sentences complete? Does each sentence have at least one subject-verb relationship?
4. Do all of the sentences have the correct end punctuation?
5. Is the paragraph fully developed, that is, does it say fully what is set forth in the topic sentence?
6. Does the paragraph have unity, that is, do all of the sentences relate specifically to the controlling idea?
7. Does the paragraph have coherence—that is, do all of the sentences flow smoothly into each other?
8. Does the paragraph use a style appropriate to the subject matter and audience?

B. List other requirements that your instructor sets forth for your writing assignments. Include such items as formal headings, formats, titles for the writings, title pages, and stylistic considerations.

1. ....
   ....

2. ....
   ....

3. ....
   ....

4. ....
   ....

5. ....
   ....

6. ....
   ....

SECTION 2

Methods of Paragraph Development

The Sampler encourages you to use expository methods. **Expository writing** is a detailed explanation of a thesis statement. The purpose of exposition is simply to explain the writer's ideas to a reader clearly. The purpose of exposition is not to make a reader *believe* the writer; the purpose is to make a reader *understand* the writer's ideas. The writer of exposition should use developmental methods.

Paragraph development means that the writer supports and discusses fully what the topic sentence proposes as a generalization. As a writer you have a choice of developmental tools. *The Sampler* discusses paragraph development by the use of **examples, contrast, comparison, analogy, statistics, definition** and **analysis**. Many times, the writer uses a combination of these methods in developing the topic sentence of the paragraph. (We will discuss the various methods of development by analysis in Section 3.)

Furthermore, some kinds of paragraph development discussed here are also expository approaches to writing essays. Thus, you could write an expository paragraph, using analysis or definition, that is a complete composition within itself, or you could incorporate an expository paragraph into a longer composition such as a five-hundred-word essay.

Development by Example

One of the easiest ways for you as a writer to support a controlling idea is by giving an example of what you mean. Examples can be either factual or fabricated, but their purpose is to develop by illustration. Also, examples may range from a few words to several hundred, the length depending on the complexity of the controlling idea.

For example, if you wanted to explain the old adage "A penny saved is a penny earned," you could give a short, personal example illustrating what happened to you and how you found this statement to be true. However, if you wanted to develop a more complicated idea, such as "the many historical attractions of San Antonio," you could discuss five or ten examples of what you mean by "historical attractions."

The following paragraphs are examples of development by example.

● *Sample Paragraphs*

Common Nouns

One of the many ways in which the English language continues to grow is by making into common nouns the names of people who were in some way connected with the discovery of something. For instance, the fourth Earl of Sandwich, who lived in England during the eighteenth century, was an incessant gambler. So that he would not need to take time from his card playing, the Earl invented a meal which would not require the usual dining implements--a dining table, plates, and utensils. Thus the word <u>sandwich</u> came to be. A second example of a word taken from a name is <u>maverick</u>. Samuel Maverick, a Texas rancher, pastured his cattle on an island in the 1840's, thus not having to follow the general custom of branding them. The word was then extended throughout the cattle industry to mean "an unbranded calf." In the latter part of the nineteenth century, the word was applied to anyone who did not fit into a particular category, usually political. Today, the word applies especially to congressmen who will wear no party's political brand.

John Mack Lynch

Words That Have Shaped American History

Many people believe that only wars, discoveries, and people have shaped American history. This is a partially false notion. Words, also, whether written or spoken, have helped to shape American history. For example, Patrick Henry, one of the most outspoken leaders of the American Revolution, made his famous speech, "Give me liberty or give me death" in March of 1775. Henry's words sparked the beginning of the Revolutionary War and resulted in American independence. Tom Paine, the most <u>influential</u> writer of the period, argued for independence in his pamphlet <u>Common Sense</u>. Paine joined Washington's army, and when the war was going badly, he wrote a series of pamphlets, <u>The Crisis</u>. The first of the series was written in a soldiers' camp after a serious setback in the war. Paine's writings encouraged the colonists to go on fighting. The next famous words were written by Julia Ward Howe during 1861, after a visit to a Union Army camp near Washington. Mrs. Howe's "Battle Hymn of the Republic" is one of the most popular and widely sung American patriotic songs ever written. Mrs. Howe was one of the leading New England reformers of Civil War days. Probably the most famous speech ever made in America was President Abraham Lincoln's "Gettysburg Address," given at the dedication of the military cemetery in Gettysburg, Pennsylvania. People everywhere came to admire these words as both a speech and as a piece of thoughtful philosophy. Last, because he is most recent, Dr. Martin Luther King, Jr., became known as a respected civil-rights leader in large part because of his powerful rhetoric. The march on Washington in August, 1963, was the occasion of Dr. King's famous speech-sermon, "I Have a Dream." By voicing his dream that some day all men will be equal, King's words join the powerful words that have changed history. Although there are many other important words that have shaped American history, these are among the more famous and important.

Beverlee Mueller

Movies and Fads

Many famous movies in the past have had a definite effect on the fads which take hold of the viewers. A recent example of such a condition can be witnessed in the box office block-buster, <u>Jaws</u>. Author Peter Benchley made the entire country shark crazy. People are hoarding everything from shark teeth to shark repellant, boosting the sagging economy of the United States and giving inflation a bite where it counts. A year ago people saw <u>The Towering Inferno</u>, <u>The Poseidon Adventure</u>, and <u>Earthquake</u>. After these movies left their scars on Americans, a craze developed for disaster games. These were soon marketed for folks who gathered around the boards to see who could survive the biggest disaster and be, therefore, declared the winner. An earlier "disaster" film, <u>Bonnie and Clyde</u>, gave birth to an incredible revival of the pin-striped suit and long skirt. This craze was renewed in 1974 by Robert Redford's wardrobe in <u>The Great Gatsby</u>. Such fads and fashions look pretty dull, however, as the movie industry jumps into UFO's and casts Dustin Hoffman as the captured Martian. Perhaps Americans will begin to build saucer-shaped homes and dye their freckles green.

Gabe Quintanilla

EXERCISES

A. Write three topic sentences that could be developed into example paragraphs.

1. ....
   ....

2. ....
   ....

3. ....
....

B. Choose any one of the three sentences that you wrote above and write a paragraph that you develop by the example method.

Development by Contrast

Developing an idea by contrast stresses the *differences* between two or more people, places, things, or abstractions. You as a writer can use either of two common organizational methods to develop a paragraph: (1) list or describe the contrasting points one by one, or (2) present one complete set of points and then present the other set of contrasting points. The following paragraphs are examples of development by contrast.

● *Sample Paragraphs*

Point-by-point organization:

Mary's dress has short sleeves, whereas Dora's dress has long sleeves. Mary's dress has a high, round neckline, while Dora's has a square, plunging one. Mary's dress has a high waist, and Dora's has none. Mary's dress has pleats and falls just below the knee; Dora's dress has no pleats and reaches only to the top of the knee.

Block organization:

Mary's dress has short sleeves, a high, round neckline, a high waist, and a pleated skirt that reaches just below the knee. On the other hand, Dora's dress has long sleeves, a square, plunging neckline, an empire waist, and a hemline that reaches only to the top of the knee.

Rock Music and Country Music

Although they provide entertainment for thousands of people, rock music and country music are different in many ways. Rock music is played very loudly; country music is soft and mellow, played mostly in a medium sound range. Rock music is a mixture of many instruments which provide a more nearly unique sound for a particular band. Basically, country-music groups are composed of guitars, drums, and a bass; the emphasis is on rhythm. Rock songs are written about a wide variety of subjects ranging from political issues to drugs; country music subjects are mostly limited to lost love, tears, beer, and trucks. Rock music is constantly changing to fit the changing atmosphere that surrounds a "progressive" audience; country music changes less and stays with the more constant aspects of life. Despite their differences, both kinds of music provide much enjoyment for many people.

Tom Jones

Flying Ants and Flying Termites

Flying ants and flying termites may look similar to an untrained eye, but they are significantly different. The ants have three distinct body segments: head, thorax, and abdomen. They have wasp-like waists. The termites have only two distinct body segments--head and thorax-abdomen--and no waist at all. The ants' wings are the same length as their bodies, whereas the termites' wings are twice as long as their bodies. Most important, the ants do not eat cellulose material (wood and wood products); therefore, they do little damage to property. On the other hand, termites do eat cellulose material; consequently, they do thousands of dollars worth of damage. Thus, their differences are exceedingly noteworthy.

Jeri Harris

Good Students and Poor Students

The variation in mental capabilities is the reason credited by many students for the difference between a good student and a poor one. However, this is the case in only a few instances.

The main difference is in the application of these mental abilities. First, the good student is consistent in class attendance. Also, once he or she gets to class, the good student is attentive and active, listening to the instructor, asking questions, and contributing to class discussions. In addition, the good student has excellent study habits. He or she does research in the library when necessary, reads each day's assignments carefully, and starts preparing for exams long before they are given. The result of this student's efforts is most often an A or a B. On the other hand, the poor student has a very poor and erratic attendance record; many times he or she is dropped from the course because of excessive cuts. When this person does honor everyone by attending class, he or she seldom pays much attention and never contributes to class discussion. If the poor student does talk, it is usually with an equally poor student. They will probably carry on a highly intellectual conversation about Alice Cooper's latest fingernail polish. The poor student's study habits are nil, but he or she will sometimes find the urge to study for an exam, most often by staying up until three or four in the morning before the quiz is to be given. When he or she does get to class and does take the test, this student is too exhausted to remember anything. The poor student's lack of effort usually results in an F. Thus, the good student learns to apply himself well, and the poor student says, "I will do it tomorrow."

Maria R. Salinas

Grandmother and Granddaughter

The woman of yesterday had a more difficult time cooking a good meal than does her granddaughter of today. Grandmother had first to go to the woodpile for fuel, maybe chopping and splitting it herself; her granddaughter doesn't have to so much as light a match when she turns on the gas or the electricity. Grandmother had to learn to cook by patient observation and painful experience; her granddaughter has books full of tested recipes, not to mention all the directions on the boxes of ready-to-cook food. Grandmother brought in her vegetables from the garden (which she probably planted and cared for herself) and cleaned them at great length under the pump; her granddaughter just steps into the supermarket. Grandmother had to run back and forth to the well-house to keep things fresh and cool, while her granddaughter has a "planned kitchen" with the refrigerator, if not the deep freeze, within reach of the stove. In spite of her handicaps, Grandmother did some mighty fine cooking, but she spent a good deal more time and energy on the job than her granddaughter does.

Frank T. Cheek

Two Dental Careers

The profession of a dental hygienist can be contrasted to that of a dental assistant. Both careers involve direct dealings with the dental patient; however, the hygienist's job is more technical than the assistant's. The hygienist is primarily concerned with cleaning the teeth and instructing the patient on how to protect them. The dental assistant aids the dentist with operations and filling and cleaning the teeth, but the assistant is not trained to do these jobs on his or her own. The dental assistant is also responsible for a large amount of office work such as keeping patients' records and keeping the books. The employment opportunities of these two professions are different also. The hygienist is able to work for more than one dentist, often choosing his own working hours and patients. On the other hand, the dental assistant works for one dentist and has an eight-to-five job. The pay for the hygienist averages about $1,000.00 a month; the dental assistant gets about $500.00 for the same pay period.

Margaret Rodgers

EXERCISES

A. Look around you and list some observations that might be material for contrast.

1. .... and ....

2. .... and ....

3. .... and ....

B. Think of other aspects of life that are different.

1. .... and ....

2. .... and ....

C. Write two possible topic sentences that would let a reader know that a paragraph will be developed by contrast.

1. ....
   ....

2. ....
   ....

D. Write a contrast paragraph.

Development by Comparison

As contrast stresses differences, comparison stresses the likenesses—the *similarities*—between two or more people, places, things, or abstractions. The comparison may be developed by the same methods of organization as the contrast. The following paragraphs are examples of development by comparison.

● *Sample Paragraphs*

Point-by-point organization:

```
     Mary's dress has short sleeves, as does Mae's dress.  Both
dresses have round necklines; both dresses are high waisted.  Each
dress has pleats in the skirt, and each hemline falls just below
the knees of the wearer.
```

Block organization:

    Blanca's dress has short sleeves, a round neckline, a high-waisted bodice, and a skirt that reaches her knees. Pam's dress also has short sleeves, a round neckline, a high-waisted bodice, and a skirt that reaches her knees.

Jim Bridger

    Although few people consider him an epic figure, Jim Bridger is comparable to many legendary heroes. Bridger roamed thousands of miles over the western part of the United States, thus making his treks similar to Odysseus' wanderings around the Mediterranean Sea for twenty years. Bridger fought many times against hopeless odds--Indians, renegade whites, animals, the elements--and survived these battles just as Beowulf survived after he fought Grendel, Grendel's dam, and won the swimming contest with Breca. Bridger amassed a great deal of money by trapping beaver, trading, and leading scouting parties, but, like Robin Hood, his generosity always led him to help the needy. And, although it is a black mark in this nation's history, Bridger was extremely instrumental in helping the whites subdue the Indians west of the Mississippi River. His work here is similar to El Cid's helping rid Spain of the Moors. Thus, a candid evaluation of Jim Bridger shows that he should rank with the best of the world's epic heroes.

                                              Amy Carson Friermeier

The Fisherman and the Hunter

    A fisherman and a hunter are two of the most comparable sportsmen out of the multitude of people who go in for sports. The fisherman will spend thousands of dollars on equipment alone.

He needs a fairly expensive rod and reel, many kinds of lures, sinkers, hooks, and accessories for his tackle box, and, in addition, he needs a vehicle not only to camp in but also to pull a boat. The fisherman will spend as much time at his sport as his personal life will allow, whether he takes a trip for a weekend at a nearby lake or a month's vacation to the Great Slave Lake to catch a record-sized muskie and mount it on his den wall. Then the fisherman will use the trophy to spend countless hours recounting to his guests his great skill in overcoming the difficulties of landing the catch. This will in turn lead to a longer story of "the one that got away." So it is with the hunter. The hunter will spend as much money on guns, ammunition, and accessories as will the fisherman. Also, good guns are only as good as the four-wheel drive vehicle to get him to the game. Unlike the fisherman, the hunter is more restricted by laws as to the amount of time he can spend hunting various animals, but this does not keep him from planning his entire year around the big hunt to Alaska. Of course, the hunter is also after a record-sized kill, and, like the fisherman, he will mount it on his den wall. When a person sees this trophy, he had better be prepared for a long discussion about the skill, daring, and fortitude with which the animal was taken. Once that story is exhausted, the hunter will launch into a longer tale about the record-sized 'possum that got away from him, mainly because someone in Gonzales County sneezed and not because the hunter in Bexar County was too excited to shoot straight.

R. G. B. Remmington

Class Registration

Registering for classes at San Antonio College is like attending "Night in Old San Antone." One's time permit is his all-important ticket for admission; the man at the door of the

Nail Technical Center is the Conservation Society's ticket-taker. Once inside the building, the "fun" begins. Getting the Master Data Card is simple, much like getting a beer--there is always plenty of it and no lines. Then the process of signing up for classes begins, and this is like trying to buy your favorite taco. You stand in line for what seems hours, and the person in front of you takes the last spot in the last class you need. How many times have you seen that delicious pile of tacos vanish before your eyes as the line gets shorter? The people handling the class cards are always properly sympathetic. They tell you such things as "Another class might open lager" ("There will be some more tacos in about three hours"); "Take a related course" ("Try one of our bologna enchiladas"); or "Take the course next semester" ("Come back next year"). One might philosophically bear up under this disappointment, but just then nature sends out a call that requires immediate attention. One desperately tries to remember seeing those "Men" and "Women" signs, spelled "ABC" at La Villeta. One asks seventy-five people before one knowledgeable soul waves vaguely to the east. A mad dash ensues, and sure enough there it is--one can always tell he's in the right line by the number of people with pain-filled eyes. Somehow, though, at both places one dazedly gets from place to place--jostling, crowding, and swearing vehemently never to return, or to at least get an earlier time permit. However, when the Alka-Seltzer finally takes effect, one stupidly tells everyone how easy it all was, or how much fun he had, or how he vows to return next time.

Jason L. McIntyre

Alcohol and Marijuana

Recent research points out several comparisons between alcohol and marijuana. Marijuana, like alcohol, exerts a continuous depression on the central nervous system. The user's "high" results from depression of higher brain centers. Neither alcohol nor marijuana is classified as a narcotic, but each is a sedative-hypnotic and psychedelic drug. They have both been known to bring about psychotic reactions in poorly developed personalities. When it is used in moderate amounts, marijuana results in memory loss, confused states, and hallucinations, as does alcohol. Both psychological dependence and tolerance develop with the use of marijuana and alcohol, but neither exerts a physiological dependence. All withdrawal symptoms are psychological. These similarities are not an argument for legalization of marijuana but only a report on the latest recognized similarities between alcohol and marijuana.

Beverlee Mueller

EXERCISES

A. Look around you and list some observations that might be material for comparison.

1. .... and ....

2. .... and ....

3. .... and ....

B. Think of other aspects of life that are comparable.

1. .... and ....

2. .... and ....

C. Write two possible sentences that would let a reader know that a paragraph will be developed by comparison.

1. ....

....

2. ....

....

D. Write one paragraph developed by comparison.

Development by Analogy

Analogy is a specific form of comparison; however, unlike literal comparison, the analogy simply uses a comparable point to develop another idea. Analogy is an extended figurative comparison. In other words, the writer compares the idea to be developed to an idea or concept that is normally dissimilar to the topic. The most common types of analogies are two figures of speech, the **simile** and the **metaphor**.

For example, if you wanted to develop the idea that conditions in a slum or ghetto are similar to those in a jungle, you could discuss how the principle of the survival of the fittest applies in each situation.

The following paragraphs are examples of development by analogy.

● *Sample Paragraphs*

Boy Meets Girl

When a boy meets a girl, she is like a book waiting to be opened and read. The cover is usually the first thing that attracts the reader, just as the physical appearance of the girl is the primary source of attraction for most boys. One should remember, however, that "You can't always judge a book by its cover." The contents should be examined. The first few pages are frequently vague, so one must read further to get an idea of what lies ahead. The first date with a girl doesn't always give the male a chance to get to know her. A couple more encounters will probably give the guy a better idea of what she is really like. After reading the first few chapters, the reader may become intensely involved and find the book difficult to put down. After a few dates with the girl, the boy may become totally infatuated with her and find staying away from her impossible. As the reader concludes the book, he may like or dislike it. He has a variety of options to choose from concerning the fate of the book. The reader may now want to keep it with him always, shelve it with the other books in his collection and refer to it once in a while, recommend it to all of his friends (but tell them to get their own copies), share it with his friends, or throw it away completely. Oddly enough, these same options also apply to the male's relationship with a girl.

Virginia Holbrook

Evolution of a Mob

The emotion and action of a mob are like a flooding river. At first, the river is quiet and still, but as the rain continues to fall day by day and the waters rise higher, it begins to build up tremendous pressure. The river is no longer quiet. There is a murmur that grows in volume, louder and louder until finally the river breaks loose and surges over its banks, gathering momentum as it goes, rolling over everything in its path, wrecking homes, killing people. When the rampage is over, the river is once more quiet and still, showing no signs of its late turmoil, unmindful of the damage it has caused. So it is with the mob. It is one of the most destructive instruments on earth when aroused. It loses all power of reason and can only follow its leaders, roaring, destroying everything in its path, until the individuality of its members reasserts itself. Then the mob begins to break up, to disperse itself. Each member, going his own way, hardly remembers what the common bond was that held them together. Even the memory of what has happened finally disappears.

Robin Otero

Growth of a Child

A child and a tree are alike in many ways. Both begin life as seeds. A tree grows tall and thick each year. A child continues to mature also. To grow well, a tree must be suited to the region where it is planted. To develop properly, a child must be reared in a suitable environment. A tree should be planted where it will have enough room when it is fully grown. A child should have enough room to play, exercise, and grow to his or her full potential. A young tree must be kept well watered until it is strongly rooted. A child must be well nourished because of his developing body. Pruning improves the shape of a tree. Discipline and education improve the child. Insects and diseases may attack a tree. A child's health is also affected by disease. In each case, proper care is needed. Much time and effort are needed in order for a tree to grow properly. So it is with the child. Both the well-cared-for, healthy tree and the child can give much pleasure to the person responsible for their growth.

Margaret Rodgers

EXERCISES

A. Write three sentences in which you create analogies (or figurative comparisons). An example might be, "Conditions in the ghetto are much like in a jungle." You might also think of a sentence pattern such as this: "X (supply your specific topic in place of X) (supply a linking verb such as *is* or *are*) like Y (supply your comparable figurative point in place of Y). For example, "Love is like the morning dew."

1. ....

   ....

2. ....

   ....

3. ....

   ....

B. Exchange your sentences with other members of the class and then develop one of the sentences that you receive into an analogy paragraph.

Development by Statistics

To develop a paragraph by statistics, think of the topic sentence as a general statement that needs support. Use numerical data to support the controlling idea of the topic sentence. The amount of statistical data used and the length of the paragraph depends on the complexity of the topic.

The effective use of statistics in a well-developed paragraph requires that you as a writer be especially aware of two things: First, the numerical data should be complete and precise. For example, do not say, "About half of the population of X City drinks polluted water." You must be precise by what is meant by "about": Is it 44.9% or 53.1%, or 49%, or what? Second, give the source of information. If the writer's data comes from a published source, then that source should be cited. For example, "The Harris Poll reports that 32% of registered Republicans feel that former President Nixon should have stayed in China"; or, "*U.S. News and World Report* states that 16.7% of the American public is oversexed"; or, "According to the University of New Mexico's Animal Husbandry Department, 38.2% of the white-faced cattle in Cochise County, Arizona, have the pinkeye." Thus, the writer using statistics should be precise with figures and give the source of the data.

Although the specific use of numbers will vary with individual, specific situations, below are some general conventions to keep in mind:

1. Any number that can be written in two words or less should be spelled out.
2. Conversely, use Arabic figures for any number that requires more than two words.
3. In using numbers with percentage, dollars, degrees, and so forth, one can use either figures or write the number if it is two words or less; however, be consistent (that is, 5% or five percent).

The following paragraphs are examples of development by statistics.

● *Sample Paragraphs*

Termite Damage

Subterranean termites are a greater threat to property than tornadoes, hurricanes, and fires combined. According to Terminix International's booklet, Subterranean Termite Control

(1977), each year termites strike more American homes and businesses than the combination of tornadoes, hurricanes, and fires. The damage to properties from storms in 1976 was $200,000,000 (30.8%). In contrast, the damage to properties from termites was $450,000,000 (69.2%). The number of properties damaged by fires in 1976 was 400,000 (18.2%). On the other hand, the number of properties damaged by termites was 1,800,000 (81.8%).

Jeri Harris

Soft Drinks, Beer, and Litter

In the last fifteen years, United States citizens who are concerned with litter have been losing a battle against the beer and beverage industry. According to Time, back in 1960 Americans drank 95% of the soft drinks and 50% of the beer from refillable bottles. These bottles could be brought back for the deposit money, and they could then be used over and over again. Today, according to the United States Bottlers Association, 79% of packaged beer and two out of three soft drinks are sold in cans and "no deposit, no return" bottles, which are used once and then thrown away. The United States is now using about sixty billion beverage throwaways a year. These cans and bottles add some nine million tons of trash to the national garbage, in this case located mostly on highways, streets and public parks and beaches. The Research Triangle Institute of North Carolina reported that in 1969 more than two billion beverage containers found their way to the nation's roadsides. Since then, the yearly totals have reached nearly three billion. Such throwaways account for 20% to 40% of the litter. A 1975 California State Health Board's study states that more than 300,000 injuries a year are caused by litter. The injuries come mainly from broken beer and soda bottles and pull-tab openers from cans. These figures seem high, but many city and state governments are fighting back to clean up this problem.

Raymond Haydel

The Price of Gold

When the price of gold reached the somewhat mystical and psychological barrier of over $200 per ounce, it caused many people to examine the history of this remarkable yellow element. According to figures published in World Coin News (August 15, 1978), the Forty-Niners panned gold for $16 an ounce. By 1933, the price for gold was fixed by law at $20.67 per ounce, and in 1934, the Gold Reserve Act set the price at $35 per ounce. This increase represents 118.7% in about eighty-five years. The $35 price remained static until April, 1968, when gold backing for the United States dollar was removed and the price went to $38 per ounce. Since then, the prices have climbed meteorically. On May 14, 1973, gold rose to $100 per ounce or a 163% increase in five years. By April, 1974, gold had reached $179.50 per ounce, but it slumped to $129 by July 4 of that year. After rather erratic highs and lows for the next two years, gold plunged to $107.75 an ounce on July 20, 1976. However, the market has steadily increased until the magical $200 per ounce was reached when the London price was fixed at $201.30 per ounce on July 28, 1978. Thus, since the Forty-Niners sold their gold for $16 an ounce, the prices have increased 1158% in about 130 years.

Beth Aarons

MISLEADING STATISTICS

Statistics can be misleading as well as informative. The following paragraph is an example.

• *Sample Paragraph*

Who Lives in San Antonio?

There are no Americans living in San Antonio, Texas. A 1971 survey by the Federal Bureau of Labor and Statistics revealed that 56.5% of San Antonio's population were Mexican-Americans. Another 10.3% were Afro-Americans, and 8.6% were Polish-Americans. German-Americans accounted for 7.9% of the population, while 4.2% were Chinese-Americans and 2.3% were Japanese-Americans. Various Scandanavian-Americans (Danes, Swedes) amounted to 4.1% of the people, and Slavic-Americans (Russians, Czechs, Bulgarians) made up the remaining 6.1% of the city's population. From these statistics one may conclude that there are no Americans living in San Antonio.

Austin Bonner

EXERCISES

A. Write three topic sentences which indicate that the paragraph will be developed, at least in part, by the use of statistics.

1. ....

....

2. ....

....

3. ....

....

B. Choose one of the sentences and support the controlling idea by using numerical data. Answer these questions for yourself: What main fact will the statistics prove (illustrate, support)? To what sources are these statistics attributable?

Development by Definition

Definition is a method of restricting, making clear, or identifying the meaning of a word or phrase. Most definitions are given briefly, usually in a sentence or less, and are usually given in the course of fulfilling some other purpose. However, depending on your purpose, a definition may require a paragraph or even an essay to illustrate clearly the meaning that you intend. Also, when your purpose is to clarify a term or phrase, you may use a variety of techniques.

Shorter definitions are called "simple" or "informal" definitions. The following are some of the most common methods of informal definitions:

1. Defining by **synonym** is probably the most-often used procedure for an informal definition. You must remember, though, that a synonym cannot be precise, because very few words in the language mean *exactly* the same thing. For example, the word *parsimony* can mean "excessive frugality," "extreme economy," "stinginess," and "tightfistedness." Each of these words has its own connotations.

2. Defining by **example** is also used for informal definitions. For instance, you could say, "Parsimony is illustrated by Silas Marner's keeping his money in a pot below the floorboards of his shack," and people will conjure up an image of Eliot's famous character hoarding his gold. Or you could say, "Blue is the color of the sky." A word of caution, though: Be sure that the example is familiar to your readers' experience.

3. Defining by **simile** or **analogy** can sometimes be used, but again, you must ensure that the reader understands the comparison. This simile could illustrate the term *parsimony:* "He is as parsimonious as a squirrel hoarding food for a frosty winter."

4. Defining by **function** or **operation** is closely related to defining by example, but be aware of the important difference. While *example* calls for a specific illustration close to the reader's experience, *function* requires putting the term into a situation and then describing it in operation. The following might serve as a definition by function: "When a person finds himself holding onto his material possessions, especially his money, excessively, then he is being parsimonious."

5. Defining by **enumeration** means breaking down or listing the parts or aspects of the term. For example, one could define "The Axis" as "Germany, Italy, and Japan during World War II." When attempting to define by enumeration, remember

that some terms are too large to enumerate. For example, one cannot define the word *reptile* by attempting to list all of the animals in that class, nor can one define *dog* by attempting to list the breed of every dog in the world.

6. Defining by **negation** is often used with positive or affirmative definitions. One of the main purposes of negation is to reject wrong ideas or oversimplified concepts. For example, one could say, "Patriotism is not obeying every law in the land," or, "A teacher is not a moralist."

7. Defining by **etymology** means that the writer traces the history of a word or phrase for the purpose of the definition. Most often, the writer's purpose is to show the change or changes that a word has gone through over a period of years. For example, "The term *bedlam* comes from a corruption of *St. Mary of Bethlehem*, a state lunatic asylum in London since 1547; thus, *bedlam* means the noise, confusion, and chaos expected from the inhabitants of the asylum and is applied to everyday life."

The **formal** definition has three steps: the term, the class or genus, and the differentia. The term to be defined is put into its genus or class and the differentia distinguishes between the word to be defined and all the other members of its class. For example, if the writer wants to formally define the word *bridge*, the word is written in this context: "A bridge is a structure spanning and providing passage over a chasm, river, or other obstacle." The words following the word *structure* (the term's class) are the differentia between a bridge and all other members of the class. One might consider this partial definition: A poem is a group of words. What other terms may also be partially defined as "a group of words?" A clause, a phrase, a novel, a letter, and many other things are groups of words; yet these are probably not poems.

The **extended** definition is used when the formal definition cannot clarify or define a term in one sentence. The extended definition, in most instances, has the formal definition as its first sentence. The rest of the paragraph or essay will then continue the differentia, often using a variety of the informal methods of definition listed above. For example, the formal definition, "A bridge is a structure spanning and providing passage over a chasm, river, or other obstacle," may not satisfy the writer. An extended definition including synonyms, examples, similes, function, enumeration, and negation may be written. Other helpful methods of defining a word are literal comparison and contrast and narration.

The following paragraphs are examples of development by definition.

● *Sample Paragraphs*

"A Bottle of Placebo, Please"

    In medicine, a placebo is a substance that contains no preventative or curative abilities for a specific ailment. The effects, if any, on the patient are purely psychological. The origin of the term <u>placebo</u> goes back to the Latin <u>placere</u>, which meant "to please". The present spelling came from the Roman Catholic Church's office of vespers for the dead. The Church's Medieval Latin liturgy began with <u>Placebo</u> <u>Domino</u> <u>in</u> <u>regione</u> <u>vivorum</u> (I shall please the Lord in the land of the living). As time passed, the medical profession adopted the term to apply to medication given merely to humor or "to please" the patient. Obviously, the patient must not know that the medication has no abilities to help the specific problem. Common examples of a placebo are salt tablets and saline injections. If this "medication" is given for dehydration, it is not a placebo. However, if a patient feels better after taking a salt tablet, and the "medication" had no known curative ability other than in the patient's head, then it would become a placebo. Other placebos are the old-time "snake oils" and "elixir," and their modern counterparts bought off of the shelf at the local drug store. These modern nonprescriptive wonder drugs supposedly cure everything from baldness to bunions; however, if a cure is effected, it is usually in the mind of the patient, not in the ingredients of the medicine. Taking a placebo is like taking a vacation after fifty grueling weeks of work. Two weeks in Acapulco should revitalize one's mind and body so that the prospect of facing another fifty weeks at the factory or at the office is not so bad. So it is with a placebo, except one doesn't have to leave town to cure that rundown feeling. A cure could cost only $2.98 at the drug store. If one buys a bottle of Supertonic, believes the label, which says "Feel great in twelve hours or double your money back," takes the medicine, gets a good night's sleep, and feels like a million dollars the next morning, then this effect must have been brought on by the tonic. Just because the tonic contains 70% alcohol, 29% water, and 1% concentrate from three exotic herbs from Outer Mongolia is beside the point.

Randy S. Gillingtine

The Noun Base

To military personnel, the word base signifies a center of operations for military units. The base usually covers a large area which contains office buildings, a hospital, a commissary, housing units, and recreational facilities for personnel and their dependents. To a chemist, however, a base is a compound which combines with an acid to form a salt. Sodium bicarbonate, present in the blood, is an important base that interacts with acids to maintain the normal pH balance of the blood. Casey Stengel would consider the word base as a denotation of one of the four corners of a baseball diamond. To a carpenter, a base would be the foundation on which the rest of the house is built. As one can see, the noun base can have many meanings, depending on the context in which it is used.

Elaine Leiser

Optimism

Optimism is a quality enabling people to take the most hopeful or cheerful view of matters possible. Basically, optimism comes in two forms. One type of optimism occurs when a person finds himself in an unfortunate situation and yet does not let himself become depressed over what has happened. Instead, he looks for what good there was in, or may come out of, the situation. The other kind of optimism is how one looks at the future. Although a job or an automobile may not be all a person wishes them to be, he simply does not quit working or driving. Instead, he hopes that in the future he will obtain a better job or car. Optimism can not only be explained by its occurrence but also by its origins in languages older than American English. The word *optimism* came into the English language from the French word *optimisme*, which derived from the Greek word *optos* (which meant "visual") and the Latin word *optimum* (which meant "best"). The word *optimism* can also be understood by observing people whose attitudes are the opposite of optimistic, that is by looking where there is a lack of optimism. Many people are constantly looking at the bad side of things. They are not optimistic; they are pessimistic.

Sylvia Ott

Clocks

A clock is an instrument that measures and indicates time. Early civilizations constructed devices that indicated time by different angles of the sun; in recent years, time has been measured and indicated by means of pointers moving over a dial. A clock is similar to a calendar that divides a year into months and days; a clock divides a day into hours, minutes, and seconds. A clock is large and ornamental, as opposed to a watch which, although ornamental, is smaller and is worn on a person's body. There are grandfather clocks that stand tall, there are wall clocks, there are table clocks. Clocks have improved greatly over the centuries. The first clocks were sun dials, water clocks, and hour glasses. Today, there are various types of clocks with intricate mechanical and electrical components.

Mary Gonzalez

EXERCISES

A. Write three topic sentences that put a term to be defined into a class.

1. ....

   ....

2. ....

   ....

3. ....

   ....

B. Write an extended definition paragraph, using as many informal definition devices as you think necessary.

SECTION 3

Paragraph Development Through Analysis

Although analysis is another method of developing a paragraph, in addition to those discussed in Section 2, there are so many different aspects of a topic by which it may be analyzed that we are devoting a separate Section to them.

Developing a paragraph by analysis requires that the writer divide the subject into its component parts. Most often, the writer develops an entire expository essay around the analysis; however, in many expositions there are one or more areas that require one or two paragraphs of analysis. Of the many types of analytical writing, the following five types are commonly used: structure, process, function, classification, cause/effect.

Analysis by Structure

Structural analysis explains the essence of something by breaking the subject down into its intrinsic parts, explaining each aspect of the subject, and showing the relationship of each part to the total structure. The following paragraphs are examples of analysis by structure.

● *Sample Paragraphs*

The Dicot Flower

A typical dicot flower (one which consists of two seed leaves, as opposed to the monocot flower which consists of only one) is composed of four intricate parts. The outermost part of the flower consists of the usually green sepal, which encloses the other parts of the bud in its earlier stages of development. Within the sepals are the familiar petals, which are often brightly colored and sweet smelling. Within the petals are the stamens, which consist of two parts: the anther (or head) and the filament (a thin stem which supports the anther). At the center of the flower is the pistil. The pistil has three components: the stigma, the style, and the ovary, which houses the ovules.

William C. Stribling

The Incandescent Lamp

The incandescent lamp is composed of then parts. The outer glass envelope, or bulb, is generally shaped similar to a pear. On the small end of this pear-shaped glass envelope, there is attached the metal base shell, which has threads formed on it to facilitate mounting the lamp in an appropriate socket. Attached to the base shell but isolated from making electrical contact with it is a solder button. Inside the glass envelope are the filament —the part that heats up and produces light when the lamp is turned on; the filament support; the button, which anchors the filament support to the button rod; the button rod, which in turn is anchored to the base shell/envelope joint; the inner leads, which connect the filament to the base shell and button; the exhaust tube, which is also anchored to the base shell/envelope connection; and, finally, the inert gas or vacuum which fills the entire envelope assembly.

Lawrence Hilderbrand

The Environment of Los Angeles

The geography around Los Angeles, California, can be divided into three distinct sections: the beaches, the hills and valleys, and the mountains. These areas are distinct because there are definite changes one encounters travelling from one area to the next. Beginning with the beaches, the western boundary of Los Angeles is the Pacific Ocean. Southern California has about three hundred miles of beaches, which vary from being wide, flat, and sandy in the South, to rocky, with high cliffs just north of Los Angeles in the Malibu area. The Coastal Mountain Range (usually referred to as the foothills) runs along parallel with the ocean, sometimes rising several hundred feet straight up from the edge of the sea in the northern section, and then cutting back inland near central Los Angeles. The foothills back out to the edge of the ocean on the way south to San Clemente and beyond to San Diego. Crossing eastward over these hills from the beach, one immediately notices the change in temperature and humidity as he leaves the cool, damp air of the Pacific and enters the dry, warmer air of the inland valleys. Especially noticeable in the summer time, it can be cold, foggy, and damp on the oceanside of these hills, and as soon as one reaches the top of the Coastal Range overlooking the inland valleys, it will clear and the air will become hot and dry. The temperature is also about 20 to 30 degrees higher than that of the beach area. Heading farther northeast across the valleys, one runs into the mountains, rising several thousand feet from the floor of the valleys. As one begins the steady climb up these mountains, one notices that the air begins to get cooler and thinner. In the winter, the tops of these mountains are covered with snow and the roads are many times impassable. The mountains are within one hundred miles of the beaches, so the changes in geography and climate are indeed noticeable.

Cynthia Packman

Musical Notation

Written music can be very confusing unless a person is familiar with the basic terms. To begin with, the staff is made up of five lines and four spaces. This is the skeleton on which the music is written. The treble clef, also called the G clef because it encircles the G line, carries the soprano and alto notes. The melody line is usually found in the treble clef. Also, the bass clef, sometimes called the F clef because its two dots surround the F line, carries the tenor, baritone, and bass notes. Harmonies are usually found here. The notes are the symbols that show what pitch is to be played or sung, and how long the pitch is to be held. First, the whole note is a circle that receives four beats in the time signature 4/4, which is the standard time signature, giving four beats to each measure and letting the quarter note have one beat. Secondly, the half note, resembling a circle with a stem, gets two beats in the same time signature. Finally, the quarter note, looking like a darkened circle with a stem, receives one beat in 4/4 time. The whole, half, and quarter notes are the basic ones to look for. Hence, music can be understood with a small amount of knowledge about the basics.

Dixie Lee Pope

EXERCISES

A. Write three topic sentences which indicate that the paragraph will be an analysis by structure.

1. ....
   ....

2. ....
   ....

3. ....
   ....

B. Choose one of the sentences and develop the paragraph by structural analysis.

Analysis by Function

Functional analysis explains how something works. The writer explains each part of the subject and how each part functions in relation to the entire thing. The following paragraphs are examples of analysis by function.

● *Sample Paragraphs*

The Small Intestine

One of the most important organs in the human body is the small intestine. The small intestine is divided into three parts: the duodenum, the jejunum, and the ileum. The first section of the small intestine is the duodenum, which is about eleven inches long. In the duodenum, the food from the stomach begins to be broken down by digestive enzymes. The second part of the small intestine is the jejunum, which is about twelve feet long. In the jejunum, the food is broken down into simple compounds, and the digestive enzymes are moved back into the duodenum. The third part of the small intestine is the ileum. The ileum is about fifteen feet long and is the most important part of the small intestine. The ileum is the part of the intestine in which the simple compounds are absorbed into the body and the blood system. The ileum pushes all the materials that cannot be used by the body into the large intesting.

Thomas Jones

The Automatic Handgun

The automatic handgun is but one of the many devices that man has included in his arsenal of weaponry. As with many of the other weapons, the handgun's primary function is to kill, either something or someone. As to how the gun itself functions, it can be divided into four parts: the frame, the barrel, the breech, and the firing mechanism. The frame is the body of the gun and includes the handle. The frame's function is to hold the other components properly together and to facilitate the handling of the weapon. The barrel, which extends prominently from the front of the frame, serves as a vessel through which the discharging bullet is expelled. The barrel provides the projectile with two important conditions. These conditions are direction, which is essential if the target is to be hit; and rifling, or a spiraling rotation, which is necessary if the bullet is not to tumble and thus alter its trajectory. The third part of the handgun is the breech. The breech is the section of the gun which contains the bullet, which is in a position to be fired. This section will contain the cartridge during discharge, permit the projectile to separate from the cartridge and enter the barrel, and discharge the spent casing. The fourth part, the firing mechanism, consists of the trigger, the hammer, and the firing pin. When the gun is cocked and ready to fire, the hammer is being held tightly against a strong spring, clear of the firing pin. The trigger is pulled, which in turn releases the hammer, permitting the spring to slam it into the firing pin. The firing pin is then propelled into the firing cap of the cartridge being held in the breech. The gun fires.

Paul Hewitt

Operation of a Computer Terminal Keyboard

Most of the actual operation of a computer terminal keyboard is done within a tiny I. C. (integrated circuit). How this integrated circuit operates with the function of the keys on the keyboard is not only important but also interesting. First, the electronic keyboard is laid out very much like that of the latest electric typewriter, plus or minus a few different keys. Each key is actually just a miniature electric switch which is merely "on" when the key is touched and "off" when it is not touched. The use of springs in each key returns it to its "off" position when not pushed in. Each key, when selected, furnishes its own unique electrical code to the integrated circuit. However, it is the function of this I. C. to condense all of the separate codes of each key into a code which must travel on just seven or eight wires to the computer. In order to achieve this great task, the I. C. must sample every one of the keys at a very fast rate of speed, or frequency. As each key is selected, the I. C. continues its cycle until it finds the next succeeding key which may be pressed. The speed of this sampling must be many, many times greater than any typist could ever type, as the I. C. must sample each and every possible key before another can be pressed. This rapid sampling process is called "multiplexing." Through the use of multiplexing, the computer can keep up with even the fastest typist with the greatest of accuracy.

William C. Stribling

EXERCISES

A. Write three topic sentences which indicate that the paragraph will be an analysis by function.

1. ....
....

2. ....
....

3. ....
....

B. Choose one of the sentences and develop the paragraph by functional analysis.

Analysis by Process

Process analysis explains the steps involved in how something is done or was done. It discusses the steps involved in completing a finished product or explains how something was accomplished. The following paragraphs are examples of analysis by process.

• *Sample Paragraphs*

Firing a Weapon

To fire a weapon is a simple task, but to shoot accurately requires practice and the following of certain basic steps. These steps are represented by the acronym "B.R.A.S.S." The "B." is for "breathing," slow and steady. Just before the shooter decides to fire a shot, a deep breath is taken. Three-fourths of the breath is then released. The remaining one-fourth is held by closing the throat. The breath should not be held for any longer than fifteen seconds. The "R." stands for "relax." The muscles, especially those in the shoulders, must be loose and relaxed; otherwise, the weapon will jerk every time the heart beats. The "A." means "aim." This is nothing more than correcting sight alignment. The "S." is for "slack." The trigger slack is taken up until resistance is felt. The final "S." is for "squeeze." The trigger is squeezed, not jerked, until the weapon fires. The weapon's firing should almost be a surprise. Breathe, Relax, Aim, Slack, and Squeeze: these steps, if followed in order, will help improve anyone's marksmanship.

Michael L. Holder

How to Be Liked

If Joe Average wants to be liked by others, he must follow a few rules. First, Joe must get to know himself. All people have their own places in the world, their own talents, duties, and destinies. Joe should be natural and develop his own talents. Joe should not attribute to himself qualities which he does not have. Second, Joe must understand other people. He must learn to take others as they are and try to get along with them in spite of their faults and failings. Joe Average should not try to change others. Third, Joe should try to correct his own faults. Fourth, he must work out a satisfactory relationship between himself and his fellow human beings. If Joe wants to be treated kindly and be appreciated, he should treat others kindly and appreciate them. Fifth, Joe should develop a sense of humor and not be too serious about himself. Finally, he should watch the tone of his voice because tone reveals many things: attitudes, character, humility, or the lack of it, and egotism. Joe should be an attentive listener and look directly at the people with whom he talks. If Joe follows these rules, many people will like him.

Deborah Foster

Soldering Electronic Components

There are just a few simple rules and steps to follow in the successful soldering of electronic components to a copper-plated, printed-circuit board. First of all, it is important that the soldering iron be of a low wattage and temperature so as not to burn up the P.C. (printed-circuit) board and components. An iron rated between 25 and 45 watts will do fine. Next, a good quality tin-and-lead-alloy solder will be needed. The most popular and useful alloy solder contains 60% tin and 40% lead. After the electronic components have been mounted on the P.C. board, you are now ready for the actual soldering--the final step. It will be necessary to keep an old damp rag handy to clean the soldering iron tip as it becomes dirty in use. Apply a small dab of solder directly to the soldering tip to aid the heating process. Shake off any excess solder from the tip. Now, apply the iron's tip to the area where the component's lead (or wire) meets with the copper on the P.C. board. Allow this area to heat up for a second; then apply the solder carefully so that it flows smoothly into the joint. When sufficient solder has melted onto the joint, remove the iron from the connection. Do not leave the iron on the connection any longer than necessary, as prolonged heat may destroy the electronic components. The completed solder joint should appear bright and shiny, indicating a well-soldered connection. If the joint appears dull and gray (or what is called a "cold" solder joint), reapply the iron for a touch up. You may need to apply another small amount of solder. Clean your soldering tip with the damp rag before proceeding to the next joint to be soldered. If you have followed these simple procedures, you are now an expert at soldering, and there may be a place for you in the growing field of electronics.

William C. Stribling

EXERCISES

Write three topic sentences which indicate that the paragraph will be an analysis by process.

1. ....
   ....

2. ....
   ....

3. ....
   ....

Choose one of the sentences and develop the paragraph by process analysis.

Analysis by Classification

Classification analysis gives an order to things by bringing them together or dividing them because of one or more characteristics. It explains how several different things are really similar because of one or more characteristics they have in common; or it discusses how things differ

Analysis by Classification

or divide from each other on the basis of one or more distinctions. The following paragraphs are examples of analysis by classification.

● *Sample Paragraphs*

Automobiles

In general, automobiles are grouped into three categories which are predominantly determined by the value of the vehicle. These three groups are the luxury car, the family car, and the compact car. The luxury group, which is obviously the most expensive, includes such distinguished names as the Lincoln Continental, the Cadillac El Dorado, the Mercedes 300SL, the Jaguar, and so on. Cars in this category are built for their plush comfort. They also provide a status symbol for a class-conscious owner. The family cars are in the midrange of the price scale and include probably the largest number of total vehicles. In this group are such makes as Ford, Chevrolet, Plymouth, Dodge, and so on. These cars are usually of the sedan variety, with a few station wagons and vans to complete the types. The compact cars are on the low end of the price range and, as the name implies, on the low end of the size range. They are smaller than the family cars but actually may be larger than some of the luxury entries. The compacts, while they first serve the needs of the family's second car and also the first car for a family of lesser means, are rapidly becoming a "personality car." Many are now being tailored to the individual's tastes and desires. This group includes such names as Maverick, Gremlin, Nova, Pacer, and so on. While all of these groups are readily distinguishable as such, many individual automobiles defy classification because of the complexity and costs of the various personal options available from the car manufacturers.

Lawrence Hilderbrand

Home Buyers

People come in many different sizes, shapes, and forms. Some are tall and skinny, some are short and fat, while others are of medium height and build. As a real estate agent, I have learned to recognize some characteristics in the buying behavior of the different sizes of people and treat each kind differently. The tall, skinny people are the hardest to sell. They want to measure everything, they never get tired of looking at every home on the inventory, and they generally find every reason imaginable for not buying. When working with short, plump people, and especially ladies, I always show the kitchen first and last. Never do I let them stand on their feet too long, and never do I mention money. The fat people, if treated right, are fairly easy to sell on a home. The easiest to sell on a home are the medium-sized people. These are beautiful people to work with because they are normally agreeable, they are most often financially able, and they rarely want to see more than a few homes before making their decision. Needless to say, these average people make the agent's life much easier.

William Barrow

Integrated Circuits

The complexity and size in the design and functions of the most popular electronic component today, the I.C. (integrated circuit), can be classified in one of three groups: S.S.I. (Small Scale Integration), M.S.I. (Medium Scale Integration), and L.S.I. (Large Scale Integration). Small Scale Integration, which has been around for a long time, is the most popular with experimenters and hobbyists because of its wide availability and relatively low cost. Small scale I.C.'s consist mainly of the simple electronic gates and flip-flops (electronic switches), buffers (miniature amplifiers), and also what are called "op amps" (a special breed of amplifiers called "operational amplifiers"). Medium Scale Integration can be described simply as a combination of Small Scale Integration I.C.'s combined into a larger package. The Medium Scale Integration will therefore handle more functions. Large Scale Integration, which is being seen more and more today, has practically no limit as to size and complexity. Large Scale Integrated circuits would include I.C.'s that make up a complete clock circuit which, with a few other components, would keep perfect time in hours, minutes, seconds, and maybe even have provisions to give the day and date. The newest Large Scale Integrated circuits on the market today are the microprocessors, or a "computer in a chip." The word "chip" is a synonym for "I.C."

William C. Stribling

EXERCISES

A. Write three topic sentences which indicate that the paragraph will be an analysis by classification.

1. ....

   ....

2. ....

   ....

3. ....

   ....

B. Choose one of the sentences and develop the paragraph by classification.

Analysis by Cause/Effect

Cause/effect analysis explains the relationship between either a cause and the effects of that cause or an effect and the causes of that effect.

CAUSE-TO-EFFECT ANALYSIS

Cause-to-effect analysis states the cause in the topic sentence and then proceeds to analyze the topic by discussing the effects of the central idea. The following paragraphs are examples of cause-to-effect analysis.

● *Sample Paragraphs*

Community Relations and Law Enforcement

Bad community relations cause at least two major problems for the policeman. First of all, the policeman cannot be effective without the help of the community in which he works. If the community doesn't help the police officer gather information on crimes and locate criminals, the crime rate goes up. This increase in crime, in turn, makes the police look very inefficient. Second, bad community relations often make the policeman's work a futile effort. For example, if the officer catches a criminal and takes him to court, the policeman may find that his witnesses are reluctant to testify because of what their friends might think of their helping the police. Thus, good community relations make for a more efficient law enforcement system.

Jim Stewart

Multiple Listing Service

The implementation of the Multiple Listing Service, a mutual listing of homes for sale by real estate companies, has had good results for small businesses, real estate salespeople, and the general selling and buying public. M.L.S. allows the small real estate business to benefit by building a large, instant inventory for a relatively small yearly fee. Also, M.L.S. brings agents and salespeople together to work for the benefit of their mutual clients and to share the commissions from the sales. Finally,

M.L.S. enables sellers of real estate to have the largest audience of buyers, while still allowing buyers to have the greatest choice of available property.

Sherry V. Danner

Computer Breakdown

A breakdown in a computer due to one single electronic component can have devastating effects on an important computer program. One integrated circuit going partially bad, or just one faulty transistor, can cause many mathematical as well as functional and printing errors. Many times, the programmer may not find or realize the fault until his program has been completely bombed (erased or wiped out of computer memory). A painstaking search for the problem may not always point to a bad component but may appear as a programming mistake. Wasted time will be spent when the programmer attempts to rework a program, only to discover that the new program bombs out just as easily as the original. Sometimes the component may become only partially bad and function intermittently. This causes difficulties only at unexpected intervals. Other smyptoms of bad components might be a completely dead computer or one that flashes its lights but will not respond to a programmer's commands. Again, this may give the illusion of a programming fault. The problems due to a faulty component or components can be one or a thousand.

William C. Stribling

EXERCISES

A. Write three topic sentences which indicate that the paragraph will be developed using cause-to-effect analysis.

1. ....
   ....
2. ....
   ....
3. ....
   ....

B. Choose one of the sentences and develop the paragraph by discussing the effect or effects of the cause stated in the topic sentence.

EFFECT-TO-CAUSE ANALYSIS
Effect-to-cause analysis states the effect in the topic sentence and then proceeds to analyze the topic by discussing the causes of that effect. The following paragraphs are examples of effect-to-cause analysis.

● *Sample Paragraphs*

Property Taxes in Bexar County

The 1975 resurvey for property taxes in Bexar County was done by the combined efforts of the city, county, and school district offices. This resurvey was a total failure, mainly because of three reasons. In the first place, there was little time to coordinate and accomplish the survey to meet various deadlines. This resulted in poor investigating and analyzing the true market values of the various properties; thus, the emphasis was on quantity and not quality. Secondly, the combined efforts of these agencies required the hiring of additional investigators, and they were poorly trained for the job of appraising property, if they were trained at all. Finally, the conflicts among the different taxing agencies hindered any progress toward a unified resurvey of property values. Most of the debating and arguing centered around procedures and priorities. As a result of these differences, more time was spent on <u>discussing</u> what should be done than on <u>doing</u> what should be done.

Leonard Yanes

Accounting No-How

I failed my college accounting course for various reasons. First, I left high school in the ninth grade to explore the world; therefore, I missed many classroom hours dealing with the subjects of math and accounting. Secondly, I have a mental aversion to anything dealing with numbers. For example, I give the checkbook to my wife and ask her to do the mathematical calculations. I then cross my fingers and hope that it will balance out. Also, since I'm in real estate and know that when I sell a home I receive a percentage of the total commission paid, I find it very embarrassing to have to ask my fellow agents to figure out how much I get. I hope that they are a trustworthy bunch. Finally, when I did take the college accounting course, the college provided the best instructor, made the best textbooks available, and sent their best tutors to help me through the course. But my feeble mind could not comprehend the smallest amount of mathematical data. Now I've purchased a Deanie Owens Realtors franchise. God help me.

William Barrow

Why Children Leave Home

A child may leave home for any number of reasons, but three seem to be more common than any others. First, a child may leave home because of a lack of parental affection, which can leave the child with emotional scars. When parents are cold and uncaring, a child senses this and feels that she/he does not belong in the home. The child will then leave, seeking a home where she/he at least feels wanted and a part of a family. Second, when a child feels that he/she is not given just recognition as a person and as an individual, he/she may sometimes feel frustrated enough to leave home--especially if the parents do not stop what they are doing long enough to really listen to him/her or at least to respect some of the child's opinions. Finally, severe punishment by a child's parents which does not suit the child's misconduct may cause a child to leave home. The severe punishment is really child abuse, and a child will normally feel that she/he is not safe in such a home. Thus, for his/her own protection, for recognition, and for affection, a child may leave home.

Mavis Watts

EXERCISES

A. Write three topic sentences which indicate that the paragraph will be developed using effect-to-cause analysis.

1. ....
   ....

2. ....
   ....

3. ....
   ....

B. Choose one of the sentences and develop the paragraph by the cause or causes of the effect stated in the topic sentence.

SECTION 4

Descriptive and Narrative Paragraphs

In this Section we will take up description and narrative. Although both are methods of developing a topic, they are different from the development methods discussed in Section 2. Also, rather than being organized around any of the methods of analysis discussed in Section 3, description is organized around space, and narrative is organized around time.

Description

The purpose of descriptive writing is to give the reader a word picture of something by developing its sensory aspects. It appeals to the reader's senses of sight, smell, touch, hearing, and taste by providing details about the subject. These details describe the specific colors, dimensions, and composition of the object or person. In sum, the writer describes the subject by appealing as often as possible to the reader's sensory perceptions. The writer therefore chooses a point at which to begin the word picture and then moves logically and smoothly through space to complete the description.

The following paragraphs are examples of descriptive writing. Both "The Old, Vacant Cabin" and "The Little Red Schoolhouse" are descriptions of buildings and their surroundings; however, a comparison of these paragraphs reveals that the first is an objective description and the second is a subjective one. In the first, the writer includes no personal judgements. She includes descriptive information that all close observers of the same site would be able to see. The second writer includes not only the information that any close observer would see but also personal judgements. Whether the paragraph is objective or subjective depends upon the individual writer's purpose; however, every writer should be aware of the kind of information (either subjective or objective) that the topic contains and tailor the approach used to fit the topic.

● *Sample Paragraphs*

The Hollerith Card

The Hollerith card is the standard "punch card" used in computers. The Hollerith card is made of a heavy paper material, frequently called "card stock." It is of a natural, off-white color and is cut into a rectangular shape having three square corners and, at the top left, one diagonal corner. The card is 7 1/2 inches wide, 3 1/4 inches high, and perhaps the thickness of a matchbook cover. On the card's face are fourteen symmetrically spaced rows of black printed numbers which extend laterally the width of the card. In four of the rows, the numbers are in sequence and ascend from 1 through 60 or 80. In the remaining rows, a single digit is repeated eighty times across the card. Each digit, 0 through 9, is exclusively represented in one of the rows which begins with zero at the top and progresses toward nine in downward, succeeding rows. Here and there a number is missing. In its place is a tiny, precise rectangular opening. These openings are sometimes parallel with each other and sometimes not. On the reverse side, the card is blank and only the tiny openings are visible.

Paul Hewitt

The Old, Vacant Cabin

The old cabin had been vacant many years. As one approached the grounds from the front drive, the first noticeable thing was a dilapidated gate precariously hanging on one rusty hinge. Once inside the gate, one became aware of the yard which was now overrun with weeds, vines, and a few wildflowers. From the gate to the front porch was a walk of about one hundred feet. The walk, which still had remnants of cobblestones, was now a dim trail of tall grasses. To the left of the walk near the house was a tall live oak, still luxuriant but badly in need of a pruning saw. On the right of the house was a long-dead hickory, with only the main trunk standing amidst fallen limbs and branches. The front porch, doorless and with a few rusty remains of screen swaying in the slight breeze, was littered with debris. Old cans and bottles, papers of every kind, and dead leaves had accumulated over the years. The front door to the house was half open and had sagged into the floor and was now immovable. The inside of the house consisted of one room, about 25 x 25 feet. On the left wall was a row of empty shelves laden with dirt. The rear wall contained one window, empty of glass. In front of the window was a large log which had been cut to form a crude seat. On the right side of the room was a single, narrow bed made of 2 x 4's and nailed to the wall. No other furniture occupied the old cabin.

Allegro Leeds

The Little Red Schoolhouse

People often talk of nostalgia in terms of places and, more specifically, buildings that they remember from their youth. The place most vivid in my mind is the little red country schoolhouse which I attended from the first through third grades. To me, the thought of my childhood days spent in this simple little school is very exciting. On the outside, there was a driveway leading from the road to the highway and back again, making a horseshoe drive. The schoolyard was surrounded by a fence to keep the kids in and the cattle out. Inside the yard, we had a slide, sandbox, merry-go-round, and, yes, even an outhouse. The ground was potted with holes with which to play marbles. A person could find more to do than recess allowed time for. When it was time to come in, the teacher would let someone pull the rope which would set the tower bell to singing. Inside the schoolhouse were worn desks behind which sat a black, wood-burning stove. Cracking and yellowing lithographs were mounted on the walls. In the front of the classroom, the teacher's desk sat atop a platform from which she taught and on which the students stood for "show and tell" time. Behind the teacher's desk was a row of cupboards in which toys and games were stored for recess time in the rain. High on top of the cupboard rested an old, black chalkboard. Since there was no running water, a nearby farmer brought in water every morning in a big jar. To me this simple little building, with its simple way of life, will always be a sweet memory.

Jerry Winger

The Barnyard

The barn and its surroundings were typical of West Texas. It had been painted that slightly sickening barn-red many years ago, but lack of care, and probably lack of money, had caused the color to blend with the oak planks to a not-quite pastel and not-quite pink. The front of the barn faced what could euphemistically be called "the ranch yard." This area consisted of a large water tank for the house, a larger water tank for the surrounding stock troughs, a five-hundred gallon gasoline tank, two pickups, assorted piles of lumber and metal, and every variety of weed (no grass) known to the Big Bend area. To the left of the barn was a large corral and a small milking pen, with stalls connected to the barn. Behind the barn was a small area designated for a garden, but mostly snakes and Johnson grass grew there. The right side of the barn was the culmination of two of the fence lines that made up the goat pasture.

Peggy L. Sanger

The Old Woman

The stooped creature hobbled along the path in front of my cabin every day at four o'clock. She always wore the same dull-brown, knee-length shawl that could have been knitted fifty or more years ago by a beginner who dropped stitches. A faded black skirt, frayed at her ankles, would swing gently in the summer breeze and cling tenaciously in the freezing winter wind. Her wrinkled face, always partially hidden by an unstarched, off-white bonnet, drooped into her clavicle. Her shawl-covered arms never contained bundles, parcels, or other objects. Despite the number of years that I spent watching her, I never knew why she haltingly placed one black-laced old brogan in front of the other as she hobbled along through the seasons of my childhood.

Dell Duncan

EXERCISE

A. The following paragraph is poorly organized, and its descriptive phrases could be more concrete. Rewrite it.

The Vacant House

The old house had been vacant many years. During this time, many changes had taken place. The driveway, which led to the house, was now a path covered by an entanglement of vines and an overgrowth of tree limbs. The house itself was an empty shell. Smoke no longer came from the crumbling chimney, and no light came from the windows. The paint on the house, which had once been white, was now chipped, faded, and yellowed. The screen door in front had fallen and was resting on the porch. The area surrounding the house had literally been taken over by nature. The yard, which had once been well kept, was now a mass of vines, weeds, and brown leaves. The flowers that had once bordered the

72 *Descriptive and Narrative Paragraphs*

house had disappeared. To the left was a fallen oak tree, dead and dried in time. The back was little more than a jungle of weeds surrounded by rotten posts that had once been part of a picket fence. Once inside the house, one had difficulty breathing because of the musty smell. Spiders freely spun their webs in the corners of the rooms. Dust from ancient windstorms covered the stair rail. The sounds and smells of life had long since abandoned this old shell.

B. Write three topic sentences for a descriptive paragraph.

1. ....
   ....

2. ....
   ....

3. ....
   ....

C. Choose one of the above sentences and develop a descriptive paragraph.

Narrative

    The purpose of any narrative is to relate, in story form, something that happened. The writer usually has a choice in telling the story: (1) narrate facts—that is, what the writer feels actually and literally happened; or (2) narrate fiction—that is, what the writer imagines *might* have happened. Examples of factual narrative are news stories, magazine articles (such as those in *Time* and *Redbook*), personal experiences, biographies, or histories. Examples of fictional narratives are jokes, allegories, ballads, tales, or novels.

    Most narrative writing in freshman English classes is used for purposes other than simply to relate a story. At times, narration is used with descriptive writing and definition, but most often it is found in exposition (explaining and informing).

The narrative should not ramble. Often, students tend to ramble about such subjects as the vacation trip they took. If one uses such a subject, the presentation must be developed around a point: My trip was frightening (narrative of the frightening aspects of the trip); my trip was boring (narrative of the boring parts); my trip was filled with unexpected hardships (narrative of the hardships). For example, the sample narrative paragraph, "A Disastrous Date" develops the topic sentence, "That date . . . with Kate really turned out to be a flop." It does not simply list several events that took place during the date.

Although many writers use techniques called **flashforward** and **flashback**, the beginning writer should start out with **sequential order**. The narrative will be presented in the time sequence in which the events occurred or, in the case of fiction, as the author imagines them occurring.

These narrative types will be treated here: historical, biographical, and personal.

THE HISTORICAL NARRATIVE
The historical narrative relates past events. The amount of time treated in the historical narrative can range from centuries to minutes to even seconds, depending on the purpose of the writer. Whatever the purpose of the writer, the events should be treated as objectively as possible. Most freshman composition courses ask students to write about a single event in history that can be treated briefly and precisely. The following paragraph is an example of historical narrative.

● *Sample Paragraph*

The Matterhorn

The Matterhorn, located on the Swiss-Italian border, is one of the world's most famous mountains. However, its history, as far as mountain climbing is concerned, is fairly recent and fairly brief. Climbers never even attempted the mountain until 1857, at which time Abbe Garret reached the 12,215 foot Tete du Lion on the southwest ridge. In 1862, Professor John Tyndall reached the 13,928 foot point now named after him, Pic Tyndall. On July 14, 1865, the 14,685 foot summit of the Matterhorn was first reached by way of the northeast arete by seven mountaineers: Edward Whymper, Reverend Charles Hudson, Robert Hadow, and Lord

Francis Douglas, all Britishers; their three guides were Michel Croz, Peter Taugwalder, and his son Peter. On the descent, four of the party fell to their deaths when the rope broke. Only Whymper and the two Taugwalders were saved. In 1879, the summit was again reached, this time by A.F. Mummery and W. Penhall. These two climbers ascended via the Zmuttgrat, the extremely dangerous northwest arete. In 1911, Mario Piacenza reached the top by climbing the most dangerous route of all, the Furggengrat on the southeast side. It was not until fairly modern times, however, that the extremely hazardous steep walls were even scaled. In 1929, F. Hermann conquered the west wall. In 1931, two brothers, Toni and Franz Schmid, climbed the treacherous north wall. Also in 1931, the south wall was ascended. Finally, in 1932, the four sides had been scaled when Enzo Bendetti, with his guides L. Carrel and M. Bich, ascended by way of the east wall. In Zermatt, a Swiss resort town facing the mountain, are the Matterhorn Museum and a cemetery testifying to the hazards of climbing mountains.

Andre S. Ernst

THE BIOGRAPHICAL NARRATIVE

The biographical narrative is the history of either the life or a segment of the life of a person. Biographical writing generally stresses three things: when something happened to a person, where the person was when it happened, and why the event is important to the biography. The following paragraph is an example of biographical narrative.

● *Sample Paragraph*

Joe Louis

Joe Louis, one of America's most famous boxers, was born Joseph Louis Barrow on May 13, 1914, near Lafayette, Alabama. In 1921, he and his family moved to Detroit, Michigan. In 1933 and 1934, Louis entered the National A.A.U. boxing tournaments; he won the light-heavyweight title in 1934. Louis turned professional on July 4, 1934, and quickly established himself as a future heavyweight contender by winning 22 straight matches, knocking out 18 of his opponents. In 1935, Louis fought Primo Carnera, a former heavyweight champion. Louis knocked out Carnera, and later won victories over other prominent fighters, such as Max Baer. Louis's career momentarily suffered when he was knocked out in June, 1936, by Max Schmeling. But Louis recovered, and on June 22, 1937, he knocked out James J. Braddock in Chicago to become world heavyweight champion. He was the youngest man, at 23, to gain the title up to that time. Louis defended his title 25 times in the next 12 years, both of which are modern boxing records. In defending his crown, he defeated such opponents as Schmeling (a one-round knockout), Tommy Farr, Tony Galento, Billy Conn, Jersey Joe Walcott, plus many others of lesser ability. Louis retired undefeated in 1949, and Ezzard Charles defeated Walcott for the title vacated by Louis. In 1950, Louis tried a comeback, but Charles won the match. He then fought and won eight more matches, but he was knocked out by Rocky Marciano on October 26, 1951. Louis's overall record is 68 wins in 71 matches, with 54 of the wins by knockouts.

Richard H. Leggett

THE PERSONAL NARRATIVE

The personal, or autobiographical, narrative tells about what happened to the writer. There are two general types of personal narrative, nonexpository and expository. We will discuss and give examples of each.

Dialogue can be worked into the personal narrative to good advantage. Dialogue, the practice of directly quoting the words of the characters who are involved in the personal narrative, adds interest and a sense of immediacy to the narration. It allows the reader to "hear" the actual speech patterns and levels of diction of the characters. Peculiar indentation and punctuation conventions are used to set up dialogue in the personal narrative.

76 Descriptive and Narrative Paragraphs

The Nonexpository Personal Narrative. In nonexpository personal narrative, the writer presents a straight narrative, starting at one point in time and progressing to another point in time. The only purpose of this type of personal narrative is to tell what happened to the writer at a given time or times. However, the straight narrative still needs a controlling idea. The following paragraphs are examples of nonexpository personal narrative.

● *Sample Paragraphs*

Bells in the Night

A telephone ringing at about 3:00 A.M. has become such a thing with me over the years that I have developed an unconscious ritual in answering Ma Bell's constant reminder of the joys of technological convenience. I'm usually conscious after the first ring. My first thought always is that maybe my wife will answer the thing and break a twenty-year habit of sleeping through everything from two tornadoes to a small-scale war. Cold reality and a soft snore tell me by the third ring that it is again my fate to sit up, throw off the covers, and somehow get my feet on the floor. Once my feet hit the cold hardwood (Why are there more early morning calls in winter than in summer?), I stand, get my bearings, and swing left. At this time, my right foot hits the dresser leg, but I bear up well despite a broken little toe. I then take three hobbling steps of which Igor and Quasimodo would be proud toward the bedroom door. I then balance my gait by kicking the left doorjamb. Two broken toes always remind me that the next time I'm going to tack more to the right and experience the feeling of two broken toes on one foot. By this time, I'm into my seventeenth curse word, normally of the four-letter variety, but sometimes, when I'm really creative, of the eight- to ten-letter kind. The words themselves are really irrelevant, but the passion behind them is next to blasphemy. By the sixth ring, I have found the hall light, and by the universally known "ring eight times and hang up," I have muttered a gutteral, roughly equivalent version of "Hello" into the phone. A slightly slurred, masculine voice then asks, "Jane?" I say, "No, George." The voice then asks, "Is this 341-1154?" and I say, "No, this is 869-8967." He says, "Sorry," and I tell the dial tone that I hope he was the unfortunate result of a faulty prophylactic used by an itinerant sheep shearer. By now, I'm fully awake, calculate the hours until the alarm goes off, drink a glass of water, return to bed, fall heavily into it with the lost hope that my wife will awake and suffer because I had to get up. Just before I martyrishly go back to sleep, I think of all the clever, evil things I'll say to her in the morning. So, in the next life, I'm going to be born about 1801, sign on a whaling ship when I'm sixteen, live life with gusto, and die very happily on March 10, 1876. Everyone thinks that's the day Alexander G. Bell did his famous "What hath God wrought?" story; in reality, Bell's first call was a wrong number to the Cruz Saddle Shop in Piedras Negras.

George Allen Simpson

A Narrow Escape

I have often wondered what should be done in the event of a rapist attack. Unfortunately, last November I found out. I was on my way to my car after enjoying a movie at Eastgate Mall, when suddenly a man jumped from behind a parked car. Grabbing me, he placed what seemed to me to be a very sharp knife in my side. He said, "If you make one sound, I will drop you on the spot. Move to your car." When we reached the car, he instructed me to unlock it and to get in. "Drive," he instructed, "down Wayside Road." Not wanting to die, I did as he told me. We had travelled for about three miles when we came to a red light. Not bothering to slow down or stop, I threaded my way past the slowing cars around me right into the intersection. I hit a car broadside. After the would-be rapist recovered a little from shock, he jumped from my car and ran away. Fast thinking saved my pride and perhaps my life; never has a fender been so well spent.

Diann Fisher

The Kill

   Ever since I can remember, I have been fascinated by the tales deer hunters exchanged during the hunting season. It wasn't until I was twenty-five years old and married that I was able to afford a rifle and a hunting trip, which I took with a friend of mine. I can still remember vividly how I felt just before the trip, full of excitement and overwhelmed with joy that a dream was finally coming true. Here was my chance to get my first deer and join the ranks of those hunters who had given me this inspiration in life. The day of the trip finally arrived, so my friend and I decided to get an early start. Upon reaching our destination, though, I found that my elation turned to bitterness because in the excitement of packing and leaving on the trip, I had forgotten my rifle. After getting over my stupidity and anger, I decided that I would just tag along with my friend and help him carry his second rifle, which was too small for deer hunting. It wasn't long before he shot his deer, which turned out to be another disappointment. My partner's hit wasn't an exact shot and merely wounded the deer. Somehow, through the brush and weeds, the deer managed to crawl from sight and we lost him. After some deliberation, we decided to separate and look for the wounded deer. Finally, after what seemed like hours of searching, I spotted the animal. One of its rear legs was torn off at the hock. Upon seeing me, he tried to leap a wire fence, but he entangled himself on the top strand and fell back. Realizing the suffering that he was going through, I knew I had to get him out of his misery. Lifting the .22 rifle (a foolishly puny weapon to use on a deer but the only one I had), I could not stop to wonder how the deer had made it this far. I aimed at the center of his skull, thinking that this would be the quickest, and pulled the trigger. I heard the bullet ricochet and go singing into the woods. The deer was now moving at a fast hobble along the fence line as I took a second aim at his heart. Before my shot's report registered in my mind, the deer went down in an explosion of dust and lay struggling there. By this time I was shaking so badly that I knew I could not shoot him again. Suddenly a third shot rang out from behind me, bringing an end to the deer's misery. I turned to see my friend's eyes triumphant with pride at his first kill. However, to this day, my contribution to that deer's death has affected me to the point that I can't even stand hunters' tales any more, much less go hunting.

Leonard Yanes

EXERCISES

A. Think of three specific things that have happened to you that could be organized into a personal narrative. Remember that you are thinking about recounting the event merely to relate what happened and not to develop an expository idea. Center around subjective narrative.

1. ....
   ....

2. ....
   ....

3. ....
   ....

B. Choose one of the above and write a personal narrative paragraph.

THE EXPOSITORY PERSONAL NARRATIVE

The second type of personal narrative is the expository personal narrative. Unlike straight, or nonexpository, personal narrative, which tells only what happened to the writer, this type of narrative has a topic sentence that sets forth the idea to be developed. The personal narrative then develops the idea. Because developing an expository idea by personal narration is closely related to developing an idea by example or illustration, you should be aware of an important difference between the two methods. A personal narrative is by its very nature subjective and has a first-person point of view. Thus, an expository idea written formally cannot be developed by this method, because formal writing requires the more objective third-person point of view. To achieve this formal approach, the writer must change the first-person point of view to a third-person one, creating an objective, rather than a personal, narrative, even though the writer may have personally experienced what he or she is writing about. In sum, if the expository idea may be developed by an informal, or general, point of view, then the writer may use a personal narrative style. If, however, the expository idea to be developed requires a formal style, then the writer should use an objective approach. (See Part I, Section 2, and Part II, Section 2, for discussions of various methods of formal exposition.) As in the nonexpository personal narrative, dialogue can be used to give flavor to the writing. The following paragraphs are examples of expository personal narrative.

● *Sample Paragraphs*

A Disastrous Date

That date last Friday with Kate really turned out to be a flop. I went to pick her up from work at 6:30 that evening. From the minute she got in my truck, I knew it was going to be an awful night. She was in the worst mood I had ever seen her in. On the way to the restaurant, she told me how bad her day had been. When we arrived at the restaurant, I didn't hesitate to get out of the truck. All during the dinner, she was complaining about a tooth that was bothering her. By now, I was ready to dump her and go on home, but, since she was my best girlfriend, I just held back my temper. After dinner, I asked her if she would like to go out dancing because it was still early. After a few minutes of convincing, she finally agreed to go. All the way to the dance hall, she was complaining about how much her feet hurt. I asked her if she would rather go home, but she said that she would make it through the night. That night I would have had a better time dancing with a two by four, but I wouldn't dare tell her that. Finally, it was time for me to take her home. When we reached her house, she didn't even give me a good night kiss. All she said to me was, "Call me tomorrow." And all I said was, "Yes." Now, that really must be love!

Bob Alvarado

The Mountain Climber

In the face of reality, dreams often change. One of my oldest dreams was to climb a mountain and to experience firsthand what goes through a person's mind after he "conquers" a mountain. One bright sunshiny morning, many months ago, I arranged to go mountain climbing with two of my friends. Envisioning myself on top of Mt. Everest, yodeling into the crisp wind, I never had a twinge of fear. As we packed our gear, I knew that I had never seen so many ropes and other gadgets, most of which I knew nothing about. I began to wonder, "Can I master all of this equipment in time?" I became nervous about the whole episode. By the time we had driven into the foothills, I wasn't sure that I wanted to climb any mountain. The hills grew into ghastly walls with long, straight vertical sides that reached the sky. I was in shock. I tried to imagine myself scaling these walls of rock, and I decided that a fly is much better adapted than I. When we reached our destination, Castle Rock, I thought of conquering castles and plundering the spoils, but there would be no reward at the top of this castle that could coax me onto its heights. As I looked up, those straight walls made me abandon my lifelong dream and keep my feet planted flatly on mother earth. I'd let the daredevils do whatever they had to do to those majestic mountains. I have too good a life to risk throwing it away for a yodel in the wind.

Jerry Winger

EXERCISES

A. Although the immediately preceding paragraph narrates an experience, the paragraph begins with a topic sentence and then explains the topic sentence. Using this same method, create your own paragraphs for the following two topic sentences or for two you write down from your own experiences:

"Although we are told that a sense of humor is an important part of a person's personality, my sense of humor is at times more burden than blessing."

"The first fortune I ever came upon left me disappointed, speechless, and broke."

B. After you have written your paragraphs, you might want to read what other students have written using these or their own topic sentences.

PART III
The Essay

Definition and History of the Essay

Because the word *essay* connotes such a wide range of meanings, a rather arbitrary definition of the word is sometimes necessary. For the purposes of this book, the word *essay* means a short prose communication of about five hundred words. Many freshman composition courses in college involve two types of essays: the personal essay and the objective essay. Although the personal essay might give the writer's personal opinions by the use of first-person point of view and other indications of a writer's direct involvement, the reader will not always find first-person personal pronouns and obvious, direct involvement. Hence, a writer may express personal opinions about some aspect of the president's foreign policy without obvious signals of that writer's involvement. Many instructors encourage their students to write the second kind of essay, thereby presenting the material as objectively as possible. An example of the objective type of essay is the one analyzing the structural aspects of the human spleen (p. 143). Third-person pronouns are used in such an essay.

Again, for the purposes of this text, the essay is a composition of about five hundred words. Generally, the essay has an introduction that states, rather than implies, a thesis, that is, a controlling idea for the composition. The introduction is then followed by three to six paragraphs that support the thesis statement (the controlling, or central, idea). Often, a short summary statement ends the essay. The designation "five hundred words" is extremely arbitrary; and the actual word length of a good composition is highly relative. In other words, one essay may require only about four hundred words for its development, while another may require more than five, six, or seven hundred words. The phrase "five-hundred-word essay" simply gives the writer an idea of how much to restrict and to control his subject.

Because there is such a multitude of compositions that in fact are essays of one form or another, it may help a writer to know some of the various classifications that are based either on the purpose or on the methods of development of an essay. An essay may be **thematic**; such essays as those on religion, governmental ideologies, and juvenile delinquency can be termed thematic. An essay may, on the other hand, be classified by mode. **Mode** is another word for method. The subject matter and the student's conviction that a particular method of development will communicate the controlling idea best determine which of the possible choices is used. *The Sampler* presents several of these modes: comparison, contrast, analysis, analogy, and so forth.

To know something about the history of the essay form may also help a writer. Historically, and probably because the term *essay* has been so broadly and loosely used, "essays" may be traced back to classical times. In Grecian literature, scholars find traces of the form in Plato's explanation of the philosophy of Socrates, and in Aristotle's treatises on various scientific and philosophical matters. The form followed by both Plato and Aristotle was that of the general dialogue, in which a real or imaginary speaker expounded the thoughts of these two men. Aristotle, especially, followed a form that is still used today: the statement of a thesis and development of an idea. Later, Roman writers such as Cicero, Aulus Gellius, and Seneca changed the dialogue form of the Grecian writers to that of an epistle (letter), written to a real or an imaginary friend.

The concept of the modern essay, however, came from the works of a sixteenth-century French writer, Michel de Montaigne. Montaigne wrote what he called *essais*, or trials. In these, he attempted to "portray himself" by revealing his ideas on various matters close to his own experiences. In 1603, John Florio translated Montaigne's writings into English. This translation gained a wide popularity and had considerable influence on English prose writers.

During the seventeenth century, the essay became a dominant genre for many writers with varying styles and subject matter. Two examples of essayists who lived during this time are Francis Bacon and Thomas Browne. Bacon helped to develop what is called the aphoristic, or utilitarian, style for the essay. Browne, on the other hand, used a more ornate style, along the lines of the classical writers.

By the eighteenth century, the essay had not only generally settled into a forerunner of the modern essay, but it had also, and just as importantly, become a suitable media for the writers' efforts. Such publications as *The Spectator*, *The Tatler*, and, later in the century,

The Rambler, were strongly instrumental in establishing the periodical as a vehicle for writers who wrote short pieces on such various subjects as politics, religion, fashion, and literature. Essayists who are associated with the above-mentioned periodicals are Joseph Addison, Richard Steele, and Samuel Johnson.

During the nineteenth century, the essay came into its own as a kind of literature. By this time, the magazine had attained a fairly wide popularity, and the essay was a natural form for the various articles on the many and varied subjects treated therein. Important Romantic essayists during the early part of the century were Charles Lamb, William Hazlitt, and Thomas De Quincey. Later, Victorian essayists were John Ruskin, Walter Pater, Thomas Huxley, and Matthew Arnold.

Thus, by the twentieth century, the essay had come into its own as one of the most important genres of nonfiction prose. However, the multitude of various functions, purposes, and styles of the essay can cause confusion when the weary student requires a precise definition. So, however arbitrary it may seem, one definition is the "five-hundred-word essay," that instructors in many college composition courses spend much time encouraging students to write.

SECTION 1

The Mechanics of the Essay

The Thesis Sentence

The single most important key to an expository essay is the thesis sentence. In most instances, the thesis sentence is the last step in the process of narrowing down the subject matter from the general topic to the specific idea about the topic you will discuss.

The first step in the process is to *choose a general topic.* These topics are usually assigned by the instructor, but sometimes the student may choose a topic with the instructor's guidance. Once the topic has been chosen, the next step is to *determine how much to restrict or limit the topic.* For most college composition courses, the topic should be limited to a specific idea that can be fully discussed in about five hundred words, or about three to five developmental paragraphs.

Once the restriction on the general topic has been made, work on the third step: to *decide on a purpose.* Formulate a purpose statement to give you the general direction that the essay will take. For example the following list shows general topics with corresponding purpose statements that could serve as starting points for five-hundred-word essays on those topics:

General Topic	*Purpose Statement*
Energy Crisis	The purpose of this paper is to discuss ways to cut electric bills.
War	I will discuss the role of the Navy's Seabees during World War II.

Government	There are several differences between Secretaries of State John Foster Dulles and Cyrus Vance.
Business	This essay will discuss the advantages of certain breeds of cattle.

After you have stated your purpose, the next step is to *evaluate and analyze the purpose* to determine what you specifically want to do in the essay. This evaluation could come in the form of a question, such as, "What idea about my purpose can I fully discuss in three to five developmental paragraphs or in about five hundred words?" In answering this question, jot down ideas for development, keeping in mind that these ideas must be controlled by a single idea and that the developmental paragraphs have to discuss parallel ideas. Often, a close examination of the purpose statement will not only suggest a central idea but also reveal a possible developmental pattern. For example, the purpose statement above, "The purpose of this paper is to discuss ways to cut electric bills," suggests that the dominant, controlling idea is "conserving electricity so that the cost of electric bills will go down." Further, the essay could be developed by enumerating methods; or it could be developed through analysis by process, explaining to the reader the steps in going about conserving energy. Once the specific controlling idea and the method and pattern of development have been chosen, you are ready to formulate the thesis sentence, the last step in the process.

The thesis sentence is the statement that expresses the central thought of an essay, just as the topic sentence expresses the central thought of a paragraph. The thesis sentence is not the title of the paper, it is not the general topic of the paper, nor is it a fragmented purpose statement. The thesis sentence is a complete sentence, either simple or complex, which clearly sets forth the purpose of the writer's essay.

In most instances, the thesis sentence is characterized by the concepts of restriction, unity, and clarity. In relation to the thesis sentence as used in most college composition courses, **restriction** generally means that the writer has limited the topic to such an extent that it can be developed in about five hundred words. This limitation is discussed above.

Another characteristic of the thesis sentence is **unity**. Just as unity in a paragraph means that the writer is controlled by a single idea about the subject, so unity in a thesis sentence means that the writer presents a single aspect of the general subject. A thesis such as "Automobile racing is both dangerous and profitable" is not unified; in order to unify the sentence, the writer would limit the subject to either "dangerous" or "profitable." Either would be acceptable for a five-hundred-word essay. Also, a thesis sentence such as "Richard

Nixon has a strong foreign policy, but his domestic policy is weak" is not unified, because it actually contains two thesis statements. In sum, to be unified, the thesis sentence must present a single idea, which will be developed in the essay.

A third characteristic of a thesis sentence is **clarity** and **preciseness**. This means that the thesis must be structured so that it is not ambiguous and does not lend itself to multiple interpretations by the reader. In general, you should avoid two things in writing a thesis sentence: First, *avoid highly abstract or vague words*. For example, "Chess is an exciting game" is not clear because of the word *exciting*. "College entrance examinations are stupid" is not precise because the word *stupid* is vague and often misused. In order to correct these ambiguities, the writer should use words that have a clear meaning, such as "Chess is an intellectually challenging game" and "College entrance examinations often defy logic." Second, *avoid figurative language* in your thesis sentence. For example, "Language is a big, red balloon burst by people with eager needles" could lend itself to many interpretations. Figures of speech are excellent expressions in and for themselves, but avoid them when preciseness and clarity are called for. The example might be changed to read, "As soon as the public accepts a rule for speaking and writing, people immediately begin to think of ways to violate the rule."

EXERCISES

A. Each of the following thesis sentences has a restriction problem; evaluate each and write an acceptable thesis:

1. There have been many important political advances in the last few years.

   ....
   ....

2. This essay will consider injuries in water skiing.

   ....
   ....

3. The qualities of a good teacher are many.

   ....
   ....

4. The morality of this country is in a terrible mess.

   ....

   ....

5. A person who wants a well-paying job should get a college education.

   ....

   ....

B. Each of the following thesis sentences has a unity problem; evaluate each and write an acceptable thesis:

1. At present in the legislature of Texas, there is much debate, pro and con, concerning the matters of legalizing parimutuel betting and of restricting the duties of Justices of the Peace.

   ....

   ....

   ....

2. Although girls mature faster than young men, their dating should not be allowed until they are fourteen; the advantages and disadvantages of this rule should be evident to anyone.

   ....

   ....

   ....

3. College is generally fun, but at times it gets boring and lonesome.

   ....

   ....

   ....

4. The San Antonio Spurs should win the NBA title, but they need another power forward; however, there is a trade in the making that should help them.

5. The Mideast crisis could have a good effect on America's economy, but the legislature is too slow in passing new armament laws and too fast in curtailing energy consumption.

C. The following sentences have clarity and preciseness problems; evaluate each and write an acceptable thesis:

1. The United States has wonderful opportunities.

2. Arnold Palmer is the Babe Ruth of golf.

3. The most exciting part of your college years will come when you join a very good fraternity.

4. Collecting coins is a very good and impressive hobby.

   ....
   ....

5. Keeping a secret is like having a million dollars and not letting anybody know it.

   ....
   ....

D. Discuss the following thesis statements:

1. Depending on the kind of fish one wants to catch, one uses artificial lures, saltwater live bait, or worms.

   ....
   ....
   ....

2. Special artificial lures are designed to be used only in salt water or fresh water, deep or shallow water.

   ....
   ....
   ....

3. Some students come to college to learn, some come to be entertained, and some come to please their parents.

   ....
   ....
   ....

The Outline

After you have chosen a topic for an expository essay, your next task is to determine what you are going to write in the paper and in what order. Before you begin to write anything, organize the material. For shorter pieces of writing—up to two paragraphs—the order of what is to be said can easily be handled in your head. Also, in some longer papers, especially narrative and description, you can usually follow either sequential or spatial order quite easily without the aid of an outline. An effective expository or persuasive paper, though, is difficult to write well without a plan for its order; thus, once you have determined the thesis for the essay, the next step is to outline the supporting material. The two most useful methods of outlining a paper are the informal, or "scratch," and the formal, which is either a topic or a sentence outline.

THE INFORMAL OUTLINE
The informal outline consists of ideas jotted down in words, phrases, and sometimes even sentences. You need pay little or no attention to numbering or lettering the divisions and subdivisions. This kind of outline is most suitable when the paper will be relatively short and when you must write the essay in class. As a result, more time can be spent on the actual composition of the paper. The following is an example of an informal outline.

● *Sample Outline*

Westerns

Proposed thesis: Most American westerns are characterized by monotonous plots, stereotyped characters, and oversimplified themes.

1. Monotonous plots--always standard situation, gunfights, chases, hero wrongly accused, spends most of plot clearing his good name.
2. Stereotyped characters--Hero, epitome of good guy, dresses and speaks well; villain, paragon of evil, dresses and speaks poorly; barmaid, "heart of gold," immoral but not really; sidekick for hero.
3. Simplified themes--cliches such as "cattle rustling doesn't pay," "good always wins out over evil," etc. Always a great deal of violence in solutions to problems; violence in relation to themes.

THE FORMAL OUTLINE

The formal outline is helpful in organizing a paper of five hundred words or more. This outline consists of words, phrases, or sentences organized by numbers and letters to show the order and importance

of the developmental ideas. You should be aware of and follow certain conventions of the formal outline: spacing, numbering and lettering, indenting, capitalizing, and punctuation. These conventions are shown in the following sample outline format and explained by the discussion of them following it.

● *Sample Outline Format*

Title

Thesis sentence: Xxx xxxx xxxxxx xxxx xxxxx xxx xx xxxx xxxx xxxxx xxx xx xxxx.

I. Xxxxx
   A. Xxxx xxxxx
      1. Xxxx
      2. Xxxxxx
      3. Xxxxxxx xxxx
   B. Xxx xxxxx
      1. Xxx
      2. Xxxxxx
         a. Xxxxxx
         b. Xxxx
         c. Xxxxxxx
   C. Xxxxxx

II. Xxxxx xxxx xxxxx
   A. Xxxxxx
   B. Xxxxx xxxxx
      1. Xxxxx
      2. Xxxxxxx
   C. Xxxxxxx
      1. Xxxxxx
         a. Xxxxx

                b. Xxxxxx
            2. Xxxxxx
        D. Xxxxxxx
            1. Xxxxx
            2. Xxxxxx xxxxx

Spacing. Center the title on the outline page. Double-space the thesis from the title, with the words *Thesis sentence* flush with the left-hand margin of the outline. Double-space Roman numeral I. from the thesis sentence. Either single-space or double-space the body of the outline.

Numbering, lettering, and *indenting.* Number and letter the outline consistently throughout. Set the main Roman-numeral heads flush with the left-hand margin. Indent the subheads (capital letters, Arabic numerals, and lowercase letters) to fall directly under the first word of the preceding head.

Capitalizing. In a topic outline, capitalize only the first word of an individual entry; however, follow general capitalization rules for names of people, names of places, titles of publications, and so forth.

In a sentence outline, capitalize the first word of the sentence. Again, follow the general rules for capitalizing.

Punctuating. In all formal outlines, place a period after each Roman numeral, capital letter, Arabic numeral, and lower-case letter. In the topic outline, do not punctuate the entries, unless the punctuation is intrinsic to the entry. In the sentence outline, punctuate all sentences as any complete sentence would be by using a period or other end punctuation, such as a question mark or exclamation point.

The basic outline format can be modified to fit the requirements of the particular writing project. We will now take up these variations.

The Topic Outline. The most common kind of formal outline is called a topic outline. It is made up of words and phrases that show the organizational plan of the paper. It serves not only the writer but also the reader as a quick reference to the major and minor subdivisions of the essay. The following is an example of this type of outline.

● *Sample Outline*

                            Westerns

Thesis sentence: Nearly all westerns are characterized by
                  monotonous plots, stereotyped characters, and
                  simplified themes.

I. Monotonous plots
   A. Stock situation points to theme
      1. Hero accused of crime
      2. Hero clears name
      3. Hero captures villain, wins girl, rides into sunset
   B. Obvious physical action
      1. Chase
      2. Fist fight
      3. Gun fight

II. Stereotyped characters
   A. Hero
      1. Speaks good English
      2. Well-dressed
      3. Paragon of virtue
   B. Villain
      1. Speaks rough, ungrammatical English
      2. Poorly dressed
      3. Epitome of evil
   C. Barmaid
      1. Immoral by occupation
      2. Heart of gold
      3. Helps the hero
   D. Hero's sidekick
      1. Older than hero
      2. Secondary in prowess
      3. Available for dirty work
      4. Provides "humor"

III. Simplified themes
   A. Themes expressed by cliches
      1. "Cattle rustling doesn't pay"
      2. "Good always triumphs over evil"
      3. "Arrogance leads to downfall; humility leads to victory"

B. Themes emphasize violence in solving problems
   1. Villain understands only a physical beating
   2. Hero can overcome villain because of God and Right

The Sentence Outline. The formal sentence outline sums up the ideas that the writer will develop in each topic and subtopic. The major advantage of the sentence outline is that it forces the writer to construct sentences that will later be used, with minor revisions, in the essay. The following is an example of this type of outline.

● *Sample Outline*

Westerns

Thesis sentence: Nearly all westerns are characterized by monotonous plots, stereotyped characters, and simplified themes.

I. The monotonous plots of the western almost always involve the same sequences.
   A. A stock situation is introduced.
      1. The hero is wrongly accused of a crime.
      2. He clears his good name.
      3. He captures the villain, wins the girl, and rides into the sunset.
   B. The plot is built around obvious physical action.
      1. The hero is involved in chases.
      2. The hero is involved in fist fights.
      3. The hero is involved in gun fights.
      4. The hero wins them all.

II. Secondly, stereotyped characters are characteristic of the western.
   A. First is the hero.
      1. He speaks good English.

2. He is well-dressed.

3. He is a paragon of virtue.

B. On the other hand is the villain.

1. He speaks rough, ungrammatical English.

2. He dresses in dark, drab, wrinkled clothes.

3. He is the epitome of general wickedness.

C. A minor stereotype is the barmaid.

1. She is immoral by occupation.

2. She has a heart of gold.

3. She risks her own safety for the hero.

D. Another minor stereotype is the hero's sidekick.

1. He is older than the hero.

2. He is secondary to the hero in prowess.

3. He is available for the dirty work.

4. He provides "humor."

III. Finally, simplified themes are characteristic of most westerns.

A. The themes are often expressed by cliches.

1. One common theme is "Cattle rustling doesn't pay."

2. Another common theme is "Good always triumphs over evil."

3. A third common theme is "Arrogance leads to downfall; humility leads to victory."

B. Many of the themes tend to emphasize violence in the solution of problems.

1. The villain seems to understand only a good physical beating.

2. The hero can and will beat hell out of the villain.

a. God is on the hero's side.

b. Right is on the hero's side.

The Topic-Sentence Outline. The topic-sentence outline is a short, formal outline that uses only the topic sentences planned for the developmental paragraphs in the essay. The writer first formulates the thesis sentence and then constructs the topic sentences for each supporting paragraph. The writer will not further subdivide the outline. The following is an example of this type of outline.

● *Sample Outline*

Westerns

Thesis sentence: Nearly all westerns are characterized by monotonous plots, stereotyped characters, and simplified themes.

I. The monotonous plots of the western almost always involve the same sequences.
II. Secondly, stereotyped characters are characteristic of the western.
III. Finally, simplified themes are characteristic of most westerns.

For an example of an essay written from the preceding outlines, see "Westerns," page 135, under Analysis by Structure in the Section 3 of this Part.

The Introductory Paragraph

The most important purpose of an introductory paragraph in an expository essay is to present the thesis to the reader. You may also use it to define a term, if the term can be defined briefly, and explain to the reader any restrictions you are placing on the thesis. Where you place the thesis in relation to the rest of the sentences in the introduction is up to you; however, the two most common places for the thesis in the introductory paragraph are at the beginning (the first sentence—specific-to-general order) and at the end the last sentence—general-to-specific order). The latter is the position most often used.

Most textbooks stress getting the reader's interest. Although this may be important, it is more important to be clear and forthright than to resort to gimmicks to catch the reader's attention.

Some of the common ways to lead the reader to the thesis by employing general-to-specific order are these:

> Present background material for your subject in the form of a helpful definition, limiting or qualifying information, or justification for writing about a particular topic at a particular time.
>
> Open with an anecdote or a quotation that is relevant to the subject.
>
> Ask a question relevant to the subject.

The following paragraphs are examples of introductory paragraphs. Identify which ones employ general-to-specific order and which use specific-to-general order.

● *Sample Paragraphs*

All Rats Are Not Alike

Recently, San Antonio, Texas, was given a federal grant in order to exterminate the above-average infestation of rats in this area. Because of the temperate climate in San Antonio, the area is an ideal one for rats to breed prolifically. This fact has created a more-than-average interest in these rodents by the people of the city. However, most people still think that all rats are alike. This is not true. There are two different species of rats--*Rattus norvegicus* (Norway rats) and *Rattus rattus* (roof rats). The Norway rat and the roof rat are significantly different. Their differences can be noted by their appearance and their preferences in living areas and food.

Jeri Harris

Romanticism

Romanticism, according to the *World Book Encyclopedia*, is a philosophy which includes the belief in the more unusual and exciting aspects of life and allows complete freedom of form.

Historically, Romanticism was neither a school nor a movement, but, rather, a restless period of experimentation in Europe following the French Revolution. It was a time of growing awareness of man as an individual, beautiful, and powerful being. The spirit of this age was so strong that the literatures of several countries reflect the Romantic influence. One of the many characteristics of Romanticism that was readily accepted by American writers was the celebration of the simple life. This celebration can be seen in the works of such American writers as Cooper, Emerson, and Thoreau.

Mimi Hennessy

The Study of English Grammar

For a number of years, the value of taking the linguistic, rather than the traditional, approach to studying grammar has been a concern of English teachers and authorities in the field. Most grammarians seem not to take a definite position, either pro or con, in relation to the relatively new linguistic approach, possibly because they have not studied linguistics in depth. There are, however, some grammarians who vehemently object to the linguistic procedure because the student would have to learn another nomenclature, because the student could not make the transition from a set of prescriptive rules to a set of rules based on common usage, and because the teachers are insecure in presenting the new approach.

Alex Galindas

Home Tape Recorders

The consumer should understand the similarities between the dynamic and the ribbon microphones as well as the functional distinctions between them before purchasing a set of microphones for a tape recorder. Shoppers for high-quality, stereophonic, home tape recorders occasionally find it puzzling, if not downright annoying, that most recorders priced above three hundred dollars do not come complete with microphones. It seems paradoxical that the more expensive the recorder, the less likely it is to have microphones, but there is a good reason for the practice of selling an expensive recorder without microphones. A pair of microphones worthy of the recording capabilities of a machine in that price range would add perhaps eighty to one hundred dollars to the price. Having paid the extra money, the consumer might later discover that the characteristics of the microphones included are not suited to the specific recording needs. Today, the crystal, ceramic, dynamic, and ribbon microphones are among the four basic types that can be purchased from just about any store that sells name-brand tape recorders; since the ceramic and crystal microphones are not generally used for high-quality recording because of practical difficulties, this paper will exclude them.

Richard Fincke

EXERCISES

A. The following introductory paragraph has a problem common to many student attempts: it has two thesis sentences, or two purposes. Find the two thesis sentences, and then rewrite the introduction, leaving the reader with a single, clear impression of what the essay will discuss.

Today's television programs put much emphasis on violence. Because of television programming, our society is being conditioned to accept violence. What appears on this mechanical monster has more effect on the actions and attitudes of viewers than anything else ever known to man. Commercials persuade the viewer to surround himself with products he may never need, political programs voice opinions to millions of people in seconds, and murder stories bring carnage into the living rooms of otherwise peaceful people. The consequences of the violence programmed are being studied today. These studies are showing that violence on television adversely affects children, criminals, disturbed people, and the general public.

B. Write three thesis sentences that you think could be developed into five-hundred-word essays.

1. ....
   ....

2. ....
   ....

3. ....
   ....

C. Write three sentences, each containing a general topic.

1. ....
   ....

2. ....
   ....

3. ....
   ....

Now, copy one of the above sentences as the first sentence in an introductory paragraph that you will write. Make your introductory paragraph contain 100 to 150 words. End your introductory paragraph with a thesis sentence.

The Summary Paragraph

Do not confuse the word *summary* with the term *conclusion*. A conclusion is an inference based on evidence that the writer has presented, or will present. In most expository papers, the thesis sentence is the conclusion, and the developmental paragraphs are the explanation and support for the conclusion. So, you should summarize briefly and precisely.

Normally, you do not need a summary paragraph for a five-hundred-word paper; however, a statement indicating that you have said what you set out to say and that you are now finished makes a more complete paper than an abrupt stop. One might compare the last paragraph of the essay to the hem of a dress and the cuffs and hems of trousers. The garments are wearable without these finishing touches, but their addition is still desirable. Often, a single statement that restates the thesis can be included as the last sentence in the last developmental paragraph. A one- or two-sentence paragraph can also be used, but all that it should do is to restate briefly what has been said in the paper.

The following are examples of summary paragraphs of student essays.

● *Sample Paragraphs*

Two Generations

Although my father's beginning and mine were different, we are basically alike. Our generations are trying to be successful and to bring up our own families in a good place to live. In the past, as in the present, both my father and I must work for the things we want. As I write this, an interesting thought comes to me about our generations. After twenty years or so, the present generation will come together with the past generation for a brief time when they can look at each other in a mature, almost objective, way, and then the next generation will come along. That new generation will view both my father and me as ancient relics of history. I only hope that future generations will find that my father's generation and mine will have left them a usable set of values and lessons from our past.

Lee Outz

Ethel Young

After interviewing Ethel Young, it is quite obvious to me that she will make her husband some clothes, that she will make more pants for her boys, that she will have an even more successful garden this year than she had last year, that she will get her degree, and that she will have or do anything else that she wants to. Ethel Young will do these things because she is willing to persistently pursue her goals and to overcome difficulties that arise. One can't judge a book by its cover; neither can one judge Ethel Young by her meek outward appearance.

Annette Long

Inflation

We now know that inflation is caused by increased production costs, increased consumer demand, and anticipated production-cost increases. We hope that this knowledge will help people learn to cope with inflation and perhaps even conquer it.

Caesar Gonzalez

Classification of Rocks

As one can see, there are many different kinds of rocks in each of the three families, and there are many ways in which rocks are formed. But all of these rocks can be classified into three different categories: igneous, sedimentary, or metamorphic.

Bart Darling

EXERCISES

A. Write a thesis statement and then write a final paragraph that you might have written if you had developed your thesis statement into a five-hundred-word essay.

B. The following paragraphs are excerpts from student essays. Only the introductory and final paragraphs of the essays are reproduced. The developing paragraphs of the essay were omitted. Make up the topic sentences that you might use to complete the essay and then write the middle paragraphs.

● *Sample Paragraphs*

Typewriting--A Skill That Pays

Typewriting is a very challenging and interesting skill to study and acquire. In years past, typewriting was strictly left to the job of the secretary or stenographer. However, in today's business world, more and more positions, both executive and non-executive, require a certain amount of typing ability. In an effort to obtain a typewriting skill that will enable one to qualify for such a business position, there are three basic steps to follow: develop accuracy at the keyboard, develop speed and coordination in the use of the fingers, and combine both the accuracy and the speed in a smooth fashion.

I. . . . .
. . . .
II. . . . .
. . . .
III. . . . .
. . . .

After obtaining the accuracy, developing the speed, and then coordinating the smooth combination of the two, the skill of typewriting will not only assist in a job-seeking effort but also in making that effort pay bigger dividends in the end.

Beverly Kneupper

Educating Children with Toys

Toys have always played an important role in the growth and development of a child. Many of today's leading toy manufacturers have designed toys for children of specific age groups. This is an advantage to one who is selecting a child's toy. In the past, toys were mainly used to keep a child entertained. In recent years, however, more emphasis is being placed upon the use of educational toys. In this society, where children are learning more rapidly than children of the past learned, it is extremely important that one select a toy that can be helpful to a child's educational process. Consequently, toy manufacturers are designing toys that can aid a child in learning to initiate action, to take care of himself, and to discover and repair breakdowns of the toy.

I. . . . .
. . . .
II. . . . .
. . . .
III. . . . .
. . . .

Selecting a child's toy should always be taken seriously. One must consider the child's age and his abilities. The wrong toy can result in the child's becoming frustrated and angered if the toy is too difficult for him to operate. But the right toy for the right child can provide hours of entertaining and learning experiences for him.

Irma Perales

SECTION 2

The Expository Essay

Exposition is a kind of writing that explains, informs, defines, or interprets. As a writer of expository essays, you generally have a choice of approaches in the explanation of a subject. Most often, your choice of an expository technique will depend largely on the subject itself and the purpose (thesis) of the essay.

The following kinds of expository essays are discussed in this book: enumeration, contrast, comparison, definition, and analysis. We will discuss the first four in this section; but because there are several different kinds of exposition by analysis, we will discuss them separately in Section 3. In actual practice, a single expository essay may use two or more of these techniques to achieve a complete exposition.

Exposition by Enumeration

Enumeration is the process of listing parts, steps, or characteristics of a single unit, or, in the case of a five-hundred-word essay, three or four aspects of the thesis sentence. Unlike analysis, which attempts to list and explain all of the parts that make up a whole unit, enumeration is simply a list of the various related aspects of one thing.

The concept of enumeration is often used in other types of writing and can be helpful in accomplishing such diversified purposes as narration, description, comparison, definition, and argument. For example, a writer could list and explain some of the historic monuments one might see on a trip to Spain, describe a few interesting aspects of the outside structure of a medieval castle, discuss three or four problems faced by private colleges, or list some of the public officials who have offices in the county courthouse. The purpose of all of these examples would be to list a few (usually three or four in a five-hundred-word essay) ideas in support of the thesis.

The following essays are examples of exposition by enumeration.

● *Sample Essays*

Tiffany's Disco

There are many different approaches to the problem of Boy Meets Girl, but, at Tiffany's, the most popular discotheque in the area, solution of this problem becomes an art. There are three basic requirements that must be mastered before one competes with or becomes an accepted member of the Tiffany's "ruling class." A person must learn the art of body language in order to communicate with the local inhabitants. This is the only language they seem to understand. It enables a person to look slightly interested without appearing too eager. Second, a person must learn to keep up with the different styles of dance that are acceptable. The person must also be daring enough to be a pace-setter when it comes to learning the varied dances that are introduced monthly. Finally, the person must dress like everybody else, yet, above all, be individual! One has to dress in a way that is so unique and "far out" that the individual costume blends with all the other costumes at Tiffany's--a cross between a Halloween costume and those in an old Bogart flick.

To be considered unique, a person must dress fashionably but not too formally. It is important to look relaxed, but at the same time the dresser must wear something that is eye catching and flashy. Generally, this means wearing feathers, sequin-studded jackets and pants, or blouses and shirts that reveal, in the light, more than their paisley print material. Hats are worn by both men and women who frequent Tiffany's because hats create moods and add touches of mystery, especially when they are cocked over one eye. The use of scarves also reveals creativity and artistry of the wearer. The experienced male will wear a very tailored, fairly conservative suit with a shirt that is slightly open at the neck. This gives the image of affluence, but at the same time gives the impression of a man who is willing and able to have fun, a combination which will attract any red-blooded, all-American female.

Another way to attract the opposite sex and to be accepted by the "regulars" at Tiffany's (those who are required to make an appearance at least four times a week) is to keep up to date with all of the new dances. This may prove to be a full time job, for whenever music is playing, the dance floor is transformed into a stage where all the participants show off their agility, balance, and, above all, their rhythm. Everyone seems to be in competition. If the male's fellow competitor proves to be no match for him, he will then go into competition with himself, trying to improve his hard-earned grace and rhythm. The female behaves slightly differently. If a girl wants to dance, but not necessarily with the person she is with, she may face toward the main body of men (usually at the bar) and dance as if she were advertising a new line of underwear. There is no set pattern or certain way to dance at Tiffany's. A dancer must simply keep in style and have enough rhythm to dance and chew gum at the same time. The brand of gum does not make any difference.

Those people who dance well seem to have a knowledge of body language, and their moves on and off the dance floor send messages to all who care to interpret them. Eye contact is vital when one is using body language. When a member of the opposite sex shows interest in the person seeking attention, the eyes play an important part. One's eyes must not appear too eager, but at the same time the attention-seeker must not be too aloof. A returned glance for just the right length of time can prove to be very effective. Also, a person must sit in a relaxed manner and avoid drinking as if one's leg is hollow. If a person acts and carries himself or herself as if he or she were handsome and beautiful, then those who probably would not give a second look will be looking with eager attention.

After one has mastered the art of body language and the proper way to dress and dance, then the person is ready to enter the world of Tiffany's where the rest is up to Fate. Once the novice has learned the fundamentals, a few tricks will begin to develop. One must remember to be eye-catching in dress by creating moods with different accessory items, to be acceptable by inventing new and creative dance steps, and to use the body, especially the eyes, to communicate. These basic requirements will insure a lifetime membership at Tiffany's, the discotheque where the problem of Boy Meets Girl becomes a challenge and the solution becomes an art.

Cindy M. Torres

Methods of Searching for Suspects

Whenever there is a crime reported and a police officer is summoned, the officer must be prepared to search for any suspects, either at the crime scene or in the general area. There are several methods of searching for suspicious people who may or may not be in the general area at the time. However, the four most common methods used by a police officer or officers are foot, spot, leapfrog, and quadrant.

The objective of the foot search is to come into the crime scene area unobserved by using all natural means of cover such as buildings, trees, or any other objects which will hide an officer and protect him from gunfire. The policeman will make frequent stops to look for any suspicious persons and to listen for any odd noises. After the officer realizes that the suspect is not around, he will then question anyone he sees who might have observed anything out of the ordinary. Residents or workers in the area may be able to help an officer find people or cars that are strange to the neighborhood. A foot search may be very effective when the officer is searching for evidence or witnesses at the scene of a crime. For example, a robber or burglar is usually looking for police cars and may be caught off guard by a policeman on foot.

A spot search is the method of placing an officer at a vantage point overlooking a street or alley which might be a possible escape route. When a policeman is assigned to this type of search, he places his car where it is not readily seen, but where it can be easily moved to pursue the suspect.

In a leapfrog search, two officers are needed. This type of search is most often used when the policemen enter a building. In leapfrog, as the name suggests, the officers will change leads. The officer in the lead covers the other officer when he takes the lead, and they slowly work their way through the building. There are many variations to this type of search. Some of the most commonly used are "zig-zag," "clover-leaf," and "criss-cross."

In the quadrant search, the area to be searched is divided into four "pie-shaped" quarters, using the crime scene as the center of all action. There will be at least one police unit in each quarter, depending on the size of the quadrant. Each unit begins at the outermost point and works its way toward the crime scene. When the units get to the center, they overlap each other's quarter and work their way back out. This is continued until the suspect is apprehended or the search is abandoned.

Any of the methods of search may be used simultaneously. Normally, a search is never restricted to the crime scene alone, as a thorough search of the entire area is needed to apprehend a suspect. Although these four types of searches are not the only ones used by policemen, they are the most common and practical.

James W. Stewart

The Problems of Working and Attending College

As the old saying goes, "A person must go to school to get a better job, and a person must work to go to school." Sometimes this is not as easy as it sounds. When a person tries to carry a standard college load of fifteen hours and at the same time to have a part-time job working from twenty to thirty hours a week, problems for that person will arise. Three of the most common of these problems are not having enough time to study, not having enough time to get the proper rest and diet, and not having enough time to relax and socialize.

First of all, there never seems to be enough time to study and do homework. Carrying a college load of fifteen hours amounts to four or five classes. This means that a student has to study a great deal in order to pass periodic quizzes and final exams. Also, there is much homework to keep up with. Usually, the student's work precludes studying for exams, so the night before a quiz finds one cramming and praying. The results are never half as good as they could have been had the student had more time. Too, homework is usually of poor content and quality because it is put off until ten minutes before class time, if it is turned in at all. The final grade is a C or D, which could have been an A or B if a little more time had been devoted to the subject.

Second, there is never enough time for the working college student to get the proper rest and diet. Running around from class to class in the morning and then going to work in the evening can be very exhausting, yet being tired does not guarantee a sound sleep. The concentration in the classroom is poor; there is no desire to take notes nor to contribute to class discussions. Also, the average daily diet of the "on the go" person is not a very healthy one. The diet usually consists of a cup of coffee or a glass of milk for breakfast; a soda, sandwich, and a bag of chips for lunch; and either nothing or a repeat of the lunch menu for supper. This poor diet contributes to the fatigue and rundown condition of the student.

The last problem of the student-worker is not having enough time to relax and socialize. There is never time for favorite relaxations such as watching television, reading a good book, and taking a long bath. There is seldom time for hobbies such as sewing or painting; nor is there time for sports such as tennis or golf. There is seldom time for dating and attending parties. Always attending college and working does not leave one with very much time for an active family and social life. Thus, a person who works and goes to school at the same time finds problems with grades, physical and mental condition, and social activities.

Nancy Billimek

EXERCISE

The following is not a specific list of enumeration topics but rather categories, items belonging to which are often enumerated in an essay. Choose one of these categories or another one, supply your own specific topic, and write an enumeration essay.

Problems
Characteristics
Advantages (or disadvantages)
Types (kinds)
Qualities
Attractions
Methods
Uses

Exposition by Contrast

Exposition by contrast stresses the *differences* between two or more things. For example, if you wanted to discuss the cultural aspects of Nigeria, you could contrast those aspects to the way of life in the United States or in another country that most of the readers of the essay are familiar with. In such a case, the main purpose of the essay is Nigeria, with the United States simply being used to clarify the main subject. However, many essays are based entirely on differences between two or more things. Here, each subject in the contrast is as important as any other—the differences between the Ford Pinto and the Chevrolet Vega, for example.

For the choices of organizational developmental techniques, review the introductory material in Part I, Section 2, "Development by Contrast."

The following essays are examples of exposition by contrast.

● *Sample Essays*

Unequal Job Opportunities for Women

"Feminist groups" have resulted from American women's protests against what they regard as "intolerable economic discrimination." In industry, in government, and in the professional world in general, women charge that they are hired last, paid least, passed over for promotions, and "held to the drudgery of routine jobs." Membership in these feminist groups ranges from the dozens to the thousands; the conservatives "go in" for leaflets and lawsuits, while the radicals resort to bra-burning and the denunciation of marriage. They are, however, both basically militant about the same things: Women, in contrast to men, are unequally treated in the field of employment.

For example, women earn unequal salaries--that is, women earn consideraly less money in contrast to men--and the gap has been widening in recent years. In 1955, the average American woman who worked full time, year round, earned $63.90 for each $100 earned by the average man. By 1960, she was earning only $60.80 for each $100 he received. By 1968, the amount was reduced to $58.20. A main reason for the wide differences in salaries is the fact that more than 63% of the 29.5 million women working today are employed as clerical, service, and sales workers, or they are employed as domestics; all are relatively low-paying jobs. On the other hand, about 68% of the men are employed as professional and technical workers, managers, proprietors, craftsmen, foremen or factory workers--jobs which pay much better than jobs women hold.

As a whole, job opportunities are unequal for women compared to those for men. A study of policies at 150 companies across the country, recently completed by the American Society for Personnel Administration and the Bureau of National Affairs, Incorporated, disclosed such unequal conditions. A full 59% of the companies still disqualify women from certain jobs, usually on the ground that physical strength is required. Still another 49% restrict working hours. In both cases state laws have been cited as the reasons. Nearly a third of the companies have work forces that are more than half female, but women are found mostly in rank-and-file office jobs. The study found that 39% of the companies have no women in management positions.

Even education and training do not necessarily bring the average woman a salary and a job comparable to a man's. In 1968, for example, a woman with four years of college was typically earning $6,694 a year, while a man with an eighth-grade education averaged a little less than $6,580. Meanwhile, the typical male college graduate earned $11,795. A recent survey by Frank S. Endicott, placement director of Northwestern University, shows no changes. Average starting salaries offered by major firms in all fields are higher for men than for women.

As of now, the statistical evidence all points in one direction: economically speaking, it is still a man's world. Now, more than ever, women are organized to end economic discrimination; how influential these women and the men who support their efforts will become remains to be seen.

Margaret Saldana

A West Texas Tragedy

During the winter of 1974-75, when unemployment in this country was at the highest peak since 1940, the Odessa-Midland, Texas, Chamber of Commerce advertised throughout the country for people to move there and work. The Chamber of Commerce also managed to get the National Broadcasting Company and *Time* magazine to run news specials on this area, a place where employment was "wide open." As a result of this advertising, thousands of poor, unemployed people poured into Midland and Odessa. Most of them had the idea that they had found "Bonanza." To their sorrow, most of them quickly discovered that working conditions in the oil fields are different from any other place.

The first difference that these people found was in the way their salary was handled. Many of these people were used to an area where if they could not draw advance pay, they were at least paid at the end of the first week. In the oil fields, it takes two to three weeks for a man to draw his first pay. Many people arrived practically destitute or with just enough money to survive for one week. The Salvation Army and every mission in the area were literally packed wall to wall with job-seeking immigrants and their families. Additionally, many people became victims of the labor contractors. The most infamous of the labor contractors owned his own hotel, cafe, and work-clothing store. Everything was sold on credit. The employee only had to give written permission to the contractor to pick up his paycheck. The employee then entered a kind of servitude. He could work his way out; however, it was a long, tedious, hard pull.

Another contrast that these people encountered was that they had to be already physically able to work. Large numbers of the job seekers were used to areas where a man was expected to be somewhat physically soft when he arrived on a new job. Normally, a man would be given some time to grow accustomed to hard, physical labor. In the oil fields, a man must be ready immediately to run tongs and break pipe for eight to sixteen hours a day. If he cannot do this, he will be replaced quickly by a stronger person.

A third difference that these people found was in housing and living conditions. It is relatively easy to find family housing in most parts of the country. However, family housing was at a premium in the West Texas oil fields, and many times, the available housing was in extremely poor condition. Often, many of the men arrived with wives and children. Even if they found employment, many times they could not find housing. They then faced the additional expense of sending their families back home.

Finally, the men found a difference in the way that they looked for a job. Most of the new arrivals were used to reading newspaper want ads and visiting the state employment commission offices to find jobs. In the oil fields, with the exception of a few highly specialized jobs, most hiring was done in bars. A man seeking employment would go to any one of several bars at 7:00 A.M. He would sip a beer until a driller, a roustabout operator, or a pipeline foreman came in looking for help. If experienced hands were not available, inexperienced help would be hired. The idea of a bar as a hiring hall was completely alien to many of those seeking jobs, and they refused to comply. This attitude, of course, set them back still further in finding employment.

Some of the job-seekers found employment right away. Some are still there. Some worked for a few months, made good money, and went home. Most, however, only compounded an already-tragic situation. Hopefully, this will not happen again. It should never happen again in the Odessa-Midland area. With the exception of a few employers, most of the local people were aghast at what their Chamber of Commerce had caused. Local pressure should prevent this from ever recurring.

W. A. Kefauver, Jr.

My Darling Daughters

As a mother, I have had a rewarding opportunity to watch two lives unfold. Loved and nourished by the same hands, these two human beings have developed into unique individuals. Both children hate schoolwork, chores, and the word <u>no</u>; both love God,

Santa Claus, and the Easter Bunny. But their similarities seem to end there. Their appearances, interests and attitudes differ a great deal.

Melissa has a plump face, set off by dimples in each cheek and surrounded by golden-blonde, naturally curly hair. She places little value on her beauty, taking it completely for granted. Brute force is usually required to make her brush her hair. She would rather hide it under a sailor hat that was given her by her uncle and play baseball. Theresa, on the other hand, has a tiny face, no dimples, and straight, brown hair. But she cares about her appearance. She will spend hours in front of the mirror brushing her hair, fussing because one side flips out while the other side curls under. She usually ends the ritual by smiling at her reflection, thinking that all the hard work has paid off; her hair is now soft, shining, and perfectly in place.

Frequently, I feel that Melissa is completely without emotion toward me when she is being scolded for doing something wrong. She usually gives me a cold, blank stare, as though she is thinking, "You don't bother me one tiny bit, Mom!" But when one member of her peer group finds some fault with her, she acts as though her whole world has crumbled. To her, their attitudes are important; mine are not. Theresa, however, hangs her head in shame when I point out her wrong-doing. The burden of guilt is greater than she can bear, and she breaks into tears as she throws her arms around my neck crying, "Mommy, I'm so -o -o sorry!" Her friends' thoughts about her seem to be of little importance. It is easy to find new playmates if the old ones are dissatisfied with her or if they are mean.

To me, contrasting Melissa and Theresa is like contrasting a rose and a carnation. They are both flowers, but their similarities become less noticeable to the observer than their differences. The rose may be the American Beauty, bright and gay, as Melissa is. Its stem is unyielding as Melissa's emotions are to me. If handled carelessly, the thorns on the stem of the rose will hurt the one who seeks to hold the rose. The carnation, like Theresa, is fragile and needs to be dealt with gently. It is not the American Beauty, but there is a special sweetness about it, as there is with Theresa. Choose which I love more--the rose or the carnation? Impossible. Choose which is better? One is not better than the other. Each one is special within itself. I feel the same about my daughters. Their differences make them unique. One could never replace the other, and no one else could ever replace either one of them.

Elaine Leiser

All Rats Are Not Alike

Recently, San Antonio, Texas, was given a federal grant in order to exterminate the above-average infestation of rats in this area. Because of the temperate climate in San Antonio, the area is an ideal one in which rats breed readily. This fact has created a more-than-average interest in these rodents by the people of the city. However, most people still think that all rats are alike. This is not true. There are two different species of rats--<u>Rattus</u> <u>norvegicus</u> (Norway rats) and <u>Rattus</u> <u>rattus</u> (roof rats). The Norway rat and the roof rat are significantly different. Their differences can be noted in their appearance and in their preferences in living areas and food.

The Norway rat is also known as the house rat, brown rat, wharf rat, sewer rat, water rat, and gray rat. It is the most widely distributed species in the United States, being found in all states. It is larger-bodied than the other species. It can be distinguished by its heavy, thick-set body, which weighs approximately 10-17 ounces. Its fur is somewhat stiff. It has small, close-set ears, which are densely covered with short hairs. Its eyes are small, and its nose is blunt. Another distinguishing feature is that its tail is shorter than its head and body together. The roof rat, on the other hand, is known as the black rat, grey-bellied rat, white-bellied rat (Alexandrine rat). The color of this rat varies considerably. The size is significantly smaller than the Norway rat, with the body light and slender and the weight approximately 8-12 ounces. Its fur is soft. Its ears are larger and almost naked; also, its eyes are larger. Its nose is pointed in contrast to the Norway rat's blunt-shaped one. Its tail is longer than its head and body as opposed to the Norway rat's shorter tail.

Norway rats prefer to travel over flat surfaces. They will frequently nest outdoors in underground burrows even when there are many suitable nesting places in adjacent buildings. They are frequently found burrowing in railroad embankments, along stream banks, under chicken houses and in corn cribs. They will, however, climb stairways, pipes, wires, and rough walls when necessary to get into a building or to find food and water. Conversely, the roof rats are excellent climbers that frequently build their nests in vines and trees. Their climbing ability and choice of the upper parts of buildings make it possible for them to live and thrive in the same area as the Norway rat.

Although all rats are omnivorous creatures, they do have specific food preferences. The Norway rats prefer food with a high carbohydrate, protein, and fat content; however, they will eat almost any available food. Their preferences are grain, such as wheat and corn; livestock feed; cereal; meat; sugar; bulbs of flowers; flour; beans, and bread. On the other hand, the roof rats prefer food with a low carbohydrate, protein, and fat content, such as succulent seeds, fresh vegetables and fruits, and potatoes. Of all the foods, fresh sweet potatoes are the most readily acceptable. However, like the Norway rat, they will eat almost anything that is available when necessary.

Perhaps the most noticeable difference in the rats is their appearance. Although their preferences of living areas and food differ, they can and will live in and on almost anything. Because of their failure to insist that their preferences be fulfilled, rats have become prolific pests for the human race to battle.

Jeri Harris

EXERCISE

For contrast topics, see the suggestions at the end of the section on comparison essays. Choose one, select a specific pair of items, events, or concepts to contrast, and write an essay using exposition by contrast.

Exposition by Comparison

Exposition by comparison stresses the *similarities* between two or more things. For example, if you wanted to discuss the terrain of Northern Mongolia, you could compare the land to a terrain that is familiar to most of the readers of the essay. Here, the main idea is Northern Mongolia, not the more familiar locale. At times, though, each item in the comparison is as important to the thesis as any other item. You might want to point up the similarities of some aspects of various philosophies of the Christian, Islamic, and Jewish faiths, for example. The following essays are examples of exposition by comparison.

● *Sample Essays*

"Framed"

Framed is almost a carbon copy of Walking Tall and has the same star, Joe Don Baker. Once again, Baker plays a nice guy two-timed by corrupt Establishment figures, and, once again, he takes a big stick in hand to fight back. This time the underworld

---

Source: Bob Polunsky, "New Movie: 'Framed' Almost a Copy," *The San Antonio Light,* April 30, 1975, p. 11D. Reprinted by permission of the author and the publisher.

comes to his aid and gives the show a different twist. For the most part, though, the character development of the hero is built much the same way; the sequences leading to violence are developed with the same pace; and the shootout at the end includes some of the same violent bits of action as seen in <u>Walking Tall</u>.

Baker is a gambler who comes home after winning a big game. He's ambushed, and the next day everyone denies having seen anything. He is "framed" and sent to jail. His bitterness grows, and he finds a friend in another inmate, John Marley. Later, he enlists Marley's help to get back at his blackmailers.

Baker's sympathetic handling of the hero maintains audience interest while the supporting cast helps him stay in the center of the stage at all times. As the main character, he grunts, groans, and fights his way to a respectable justice, and it is his sincerity that keeps the film above board. As in <u>Walking Tall</u>, Baker's likability keeps the audience rooting for him.

Connie van Dyke, the pretty blonde from <u>W. W. and the Dixie Dancekings</u>, is Baker's girl. During most of the show, he believes she is involved with the blackmailers, and Miss van Dyke makes the unpredictable personality of the girl memorable. Brock Peters scores as a staunch, law-abiding black cop, and Gabriel Dell turns in a colorful performance as a criminal. Dell appeared in many Dead End Kids features of the past; so this role is almost a nostalgic piece for him.

Bob Polunsky

Professional and Volunteer Ambulance Services

Ambulance associations are needed by communities both large and small. Whether they are professional or volunteer, the services rendered by these associations are a vital lifeline for many people each year. There are sometimes individual differences between one or more associations; however, the similarities between volunteer and professional ambulance associations are shown in their basic set-ups, their training programs, and their equipment.

The first similarity between volunteer and professional ambulance associations is that both have an official charter which is certified by the state. The charter has in it the various rules and regulations of both statewide and local organizations. The volunteer associations and the professional associations have officers elected by the members, business meetings set up for at least once a month, and practice meetings set up for one or more times a month. Both organizations find it necessary to continue practicing and learning the various skills needed to be adequately trained for duty.

Also, training programs are established for both types of organizations, usually as a joint effort by several counties. Basic Red Cross is a prerequisite for any ambulance association member. This Red Cross trainee learns skills involved in basic first aid. The course takes from twelve to fifteen hours to complete, and the training is valid for three years. The next step both volunteer and professional ambulance association members must complete is the Emergency Care Attendance course. In this twenty- to twenty-four-hour class, more intricately vital knowledge is learned. Instead of just the simple splinting and bandaging of Basic Red Cross, many more complicated procedures such as birth, cardiopulmonary resuscitation, and major disaster aid are taught. This training is valid for two to three years for members of each association. The highest form of simple emergency learning available for members of both organizations is the Emergency Medical Technician course. The EMT learns everything from splinting a broken arm to starting intravenous feedings. The EMT training is, or should be, the goal of every ambulance attendant.

The equipment for both professional and volunteer ambulances is essentially the same. Each organization is equipped with an ambulance or modulance—complete with identification, flashing lights, and sirens. Most associations also have a back-up unit. The ambulances of both associations contain basic first aid items such as splints, bandages, and antiseptic, supplies of oxygen, and at least one regular stretcher and one cot-type portable stretcher. In addition to this basic equipment, both organizations' ambulances are supplied with long and short backboards, traction splints, at least one obstetrical kit, and sometimes a respirator. Also important to the functioning of both ambulance services is the communications equipment. To receive the emergency calls in the first place, there are scanners or plectrons that sound off. These devices tell the location and sometimes even the type of emergency. Also, for the reports, there is a two-way radio system for ambulance-to-sheriff's-office and ambulance-to-hospital communication. In addition to these systems, both volunteer and professional ambulances are many times equipped with a phone for ambulance-to-emergency-room contact. Vital information concerning the care for a patient will be given directly and quickly with no interference. With this phone, professional and volunteer ambulance associations will be able to give the complete vital care and have the voice of a doctor or registered nurse to fill in any gap in knowledge necessary to the well-being of that patient.

Toni Trouart

EXERCISE

The following topics may be used for either comparison or contrast, and sometimes both:

Infatuation and love

College and high school (limit the comparison or contrast to teachers, subjects, administrators, extracurricular activities, student behavior)

Two geographic locations (cities, terrains, rivers)

Two automobiles (American, foreign, compacts, full-sized)

Two people (personal friends, relatives, politicians, actors, pets)

You and your parent(s) (attitudes, opportunities, interests, personalities)

Two television shows (situation comedies, detectives, cowboys, talk shows, network news)

Two cultures (social ideas, moral ideas, customs)

Choose one of these general topics (or another one that you can think of), select specific items for comparison, if necessary, and write an essay using exposition by comparison.

Exposition by Definition

An extended, formal definition is the process of defining a word, term, phrase, or concept beyond the general uses of a simple or informal definition. This kind of exposition is usually a purpose unto itself, that is, the writer is defining a term not in order to discuss another topic but to clarify the use and concept of that term.

For example, in a paper entitled "The Immorality of the Viet Nam War," a writer may briefly define the word *immorality* and then discuss the ideas about the war and how the definition applies to the war. But a paper entitled "What is Immorality?" is another kind of paper. This definition essay may devote itself to discussing the meaning of the word *immorality* as a concept.

The extended-definition essay usually makes use of several expository techniques, such as enumeration, example, function, classification, and comparison or contrast. It may also use the informal definition devices such as synonym, negation, and etymology to develop the writer's purpose.

The following essays are examples of exposition by definition.

● *Sample Essays*

Brandy

The adage "A Rose by any other name" may apply to a great many things in life. However, when one is around experts in particular subjects, such as roses, then a rose is not a rose, but R. hugonis, R. chinensis, or R. moschata. So it is with connoisseurs of alcoholic beverages. Perhaps a discussion of the common term <u>brandy</u> will illustrate this point and keep one from feeling like a klutz the next time some "expert" gives a forty-five-minute treatise on the subject.

Basically, brandy, known in Latin as <u>spiritus</u> <u>vini</u> <u>vitis</u>, or spirit of the wine of life, is an alcoholic liquid (wine) made by distilling the fermented juice of ripe grapes. Brandy, originally brandywine, came from the Dutch and French languages and literally translated meant "burnt wine" (<u>branden</u> <u>wign</u>), with "burnt" being a general synonym for "distill." The finest brandy is usually considered to be cognac, which comes from a region in Western France by that name. Only brandies distilled in this district may be called "cognac." Other common brandies are armagnac, from the Armagnac region of France; Spanish brandy, from Spain; Metaxa, from Greece; Grappa, from Italy; and California brandy, from the United States.

Also, wine made by fermenting other fruits such as oranges, peaches, and pears can be distilled to make brandy. These products are true brandies, but they will use a qualifying adjective in the name, such as "peach brandy." Common brandies using a fermented base other than grapes are apple brandy, sometimes called "applejack" and known as "Calvados" in France; plum brandy, known variously as "quetsch," "mirabelle," and "slivovitz"; cherry brandy, called "kirsch" in Germany; and raspberry brandy, called "framboise."

The production of cognac can serve as an example for the process of making any brandy. First, the base for cognac is a sour white wine containing about seventy percent alcohol. Cognac is then distilled in a pot still and stored in oak barrels. During storage, cognac takes on some color and loses some of its alcoholic content. At the same time, it becomes smoother and develops a bouquet. After five years of storage, the cognac has about sixty-five percent alcohol content. It is then blended with older cognac and diluted with water to around forty-five percent alcohol. The cognac is colored with caramel and is then ready for the market.

Although the terms <u>liqueur</u> and <u>cordial</u> are sometimes used synonymously with <u>brandy</u>, they are not brandy. The distinction between a brandy and a liqueur or cordial is mainly in the distillation process. Brandy is made by distilling the fermented juice of a fruit, whereas a liqueur or cordial is produced by adding fruits, spices or other flavorings to an already distilled liquor, such as a brandy or grain alcohol. The general distinction between a liqueur and a cordial is that liqueurs usually add spices to the alcoholic base, and cordials usually add fruits to the alcoholic base. Although brandies, liqueurs, and cordials are all considered "after dinner" drinks, a further distinction between them lies in the way they are served. Brandy may be served in a small glass, but normally a small amount is served in a brandy snifter; liqueurs and cordials are usually served in a one-ounce "pony," or liqueur glass. Many times, all of these are served with coffee.

To the medical profession, brandy is classified as one of a group of alcoholic drugs which dilates the surface blood vessels, increases circulation of the blood, and produces drowsiness; therefore, brandy has a sedative effect. However, the medical profession's definition of brandy is obviously too clinical. Most often, brandy is associated with a romantic setting by the fireplace on a cold winter night. When one is enjoying the fire and one's favorite person, one should also enjoy the mellow sensation of a fine brandy going down smoothly for an evening of enchantment and love.

Charles Long

Courage

Courage is a quality enabling people to conquer fear or despair. This is what anybody would find by looking up the word <u>courage</u> in the dictionary. Yet what is it that makes a person known as "courageous"? Just what is "courage"?

The word <u>courage</u> originates in Middle English, Old French, and Latin. <u>Coer</u>, which is Old French, meant "heart, that which contains emotions." The Middle English version of the word was <u>corage</u>, which meant "heart as the seat of feelings." Both the Old French and Middle English versions of the word evolved from the Latin <u>cor</u>, which simply meant "heart." Even though courage has its roots in past languages, its meaning has not undergone drastic changes over the years. Today, courage is still a quality associated with the deep, inner feelings of a person. Many synonyms which also are associated with emotions take on the connotation of courage. A few such words are <u>bravery</u>, <u>fearlessness</u>, <u>valor</u>, and <u>boldness</u>.

    A person can look up the definition and origin of the word and acquire a fair understanding of the abstract concept of the word. Yet the word has no real effect until it is seen in action. Courage can be seen in a soldier who risks his life in the line of duty for another person or for his country. An example of this kind of courageous person would be Audie Murphy, the most decorated American soldier of World War II. However, courage is not necessarily shown in such an obvious way. Anyone who faces a difficult problem in life optimistically can be said to be courageous. An example of this kind of courage would be Martin Luther King, Jr. because of his nonviolent philosophy and his undaunted belief in his "dream."

    One can also better understand what courage is by seeing what it is not. A soldier who acts cowardly because he cannot control his fear is certainly not courageous. Even in daily living, some people cannot find the courage to look at tomorrow optimistically. Thus, a soldier or an average person who cannot control fear of a situation is anything but courageous.

    Courage is also closely associated with one of man's most prized emotions, love. The courage required here is for one to be able to trust in someone enough to give of oneself. In this instance, courage thus requires selflessness, a quality also seen in Audie Murphy's bravery on the battlefield and Martin Luther King's fearlessness in a predominately white society.

So, courage, like all abstract terms, is difficult to fully understand until it is manifested in a tangible, often physical, action.

Sylvia Ott

Machismo

The term machismo often brings to mind flattering images of an able-bodied man who exhibits, usually without effort, desirable qualities such as self-assurance, independence, and skilled proficiency in most situations. However appealing these qualities might appear on the surface, a closer look into the personality behind them usually reveals a biased sense of masculine pride that quickly becomes domineering and arrogant. Machismo is an exaggerated awareness and strong assertion of masculinity which is often aggressive in nature. Because of the obvious misconceptions which have been associated with this quality, it is necessary to point out many of the undesirable traits and thus gain a clearer picture of the true concept of machismo.

Machismo is, indeed, very closely related to masculinity; however, masculinity involves having qualities appropriate to man, whereas machismo involves merely using these qualities, often to an excess. A male who is confident rarely finds it necessary to resort to machismo, because his masculinity is a characteristic of his personality with which he is comfortable. On the other hand, a man who feels a constant need to assure himself of his masculinity often assumes the manner of an agressively virile man.

Because of the close association between machismo and masculinity, it is difficult to cite specific examples which illustrate either quality exclusively. The attitude expressed in a situation would help determine the distinction, although one may not rely entirely on this. A man who refuses to cry because he feels it would not be masculine would appropriately illustrate foolish machismo. One has only to look at the photographs of miners, exhausted and black with coal dust, who have been working around the clock to save trapped workers to know that brave, masculine males do indeed cry. The silent tears that wash clean the dirty cheeks of these miners whose friends could not be rescued are mute testimony to belie the idea that a real man doesn't cry.

Machismo, sometimes more commonly referred to as macho, is also used as a device for gaining attention, often of the opposite sex. Men who deliberately lower their voices, display an attitude of supreme superiority, or attempt to impress by the use of their brute strength may be illustrating their concept of macho. A true man of strength may never need to push over a temple. There is aura about him that suggests his potential.

While machismo is frequently used to command attention, it is also used to indicate authority or domination. A strong, virile personality and an ability to deal authoritatively with affairs are supposedly traits of a man who possesses machismo. However, proficiency and skill are qualities which are often absent, and the strong personality and authoritarian bearing may be merely showy pretenses.

Machismo has also been used as a substitute for male charisma. The two terms are often used synonymously, although the use is incorrect. A man with charisma possesses a special magnetic charm and appeal, and this quality certainly may not be duplicated by the use of meager machismo.

Although it is certainly true that machismo may be temporarily appealing in a few instances, it will never replace the subtleness of true masculinity or male charisma.

Tina Stains

Happiness

The word <u>happiness</u> generally suggests a feeling of great pleasure, contentment, and joy. This is information anybody finds by looking up the word in a dictionary. Yet what is it that makes a person happy? Just what <u>is</u> "happiness"?

The word originated in the French and Italian languages. <u>Bonheur</u>, which is French, literally means "happiness of the day." The Italian version of the word is <u>felicita</u>, which means "to make happy." Even though these words for happiness came into the languages long ago, the meaning of the word has not undergone any drastic changes over the years. Today, happiness is still a feeling associated with the inner feelings of a person. Many synonyms which are associated with feelings connote happiness. A few such words are <u>cheer</u>, <u>gladness</u>, and <u>joyfulness</u>.

It is difficult to say exactly what happiness is, but we all know it when we feel it, and we all know when we are feeling happy. We also know what it is not. People who are sad or miserable with their lives know that there is a general feeling of discomfort that is definitely not happiness within them.

Happiness is to a person like a ball of string is to a kitten. It is a source of pleasurable stimulation, bliss, felicity, and contentment, all mixed up with an active or passive state of pleasure.

Being happy is different from having fun; it is not the same as enjoying life. People can go places, do things, see all they can, enjoy sex, leisure, good company, music, plays, liquor, tobacco, dancing, entertainment, and even work; they can have plenty of money; however, if they are not <u>content</u> with their lives, they are not happy.

Happiness is also closely <u>associated</u> with that most prized feeling--satisfaction. The happiness here is the feeling of fulfilling the desires, expectations, needs, and demands of the individual. For example, a person content with his or her surroundings can be a happy person.

So, happiness, like all abstract terms, is difficult to fully describe because it is an intangible feeling. People usually can not explain happiness, but they know when they are happy.

Deborah Foster

EXERCISE

The following suggestions are subdivided into concrete and abstract terms; choose one from each group and write an extended definition.

Concrete Terms	*Abstract Terms*
Barbershop quartet	Corruption
Black sheep	Sophistication
Red tape	Patriotism
Escargots bourguignonne	Justice
Idol	Obscenity
Village	Jealousy
Yankee	Etiquette
Jersey (cloth)	Extremism
Beer	Gusto

SECTION 3

The Analytical Essay

Analysis is a method of developing an idea by which the writer divides the subject into its component parts. It is thus a method of exposition; however, because there are several different types of exposition by analysis, we will discuss them separately in this section. Unlike enumeration, however, analysis must not only list and explain the individual segments of the whole but also explain the relationships, if any, between the segments themselves.

Analysis by Structure

Structural analysis is a method of explaining the nature of something. To do this, the writer breaks down the subject into the qualities, characteristics, or segments that make up the entity. For example, the working force of a college is generally divided into three distinct elements—the administration, the faculty, and the staff; or, the structure of most fictional prose involves theme, plot, and character.

Frequently, the explanation of a structure will involve the use of description, function, comparison, and contrast.

The following essays are examples of analysis by structure.

● *Sample Essays*

Westerns

Many times things repeat themselves for the better, but this doesn't seem to apply to the popular fiction that is found in the book stores. Most popular fiction, such as detective stories, spy stories, and science fiction stories, are pretty much the same, but the authors will usually vary them and update them enough to make them at least readable. However, this doesn't seem to apply to the typical Western story. The adage "If you've seen one you've seen them all" is almost literally true, mainly because nearly all westerns are characterized by monotonous plots, stereotyped characters, and simplified themes.

The monotonous plots of the western almost always involve the same sequence: First, a stock situation is introduced that will ultimately point to the theme of the story. Always, it seems, the hero is wrongly accused of a heinous crime. He then spends the rest of the story clearing his good name. At the end, he will invariably capture the villain, win the girl he loves, and ride off into the sunset. Also, the plot is built around obvious physical action. The hero is involved in numerous chases, fist fights, and gun fights, all of which he wins.

Second, stereotyped characters are characteristic of the western. First, and most important, is the hero. He speaks good English, is well-dressed (usually in light colors), and his moral bearing says that he is the paragon of virtue. On the other hand is the villain. He speaks rough, ungrammatical English, dresses in dark, drab, wrinkled clothes, and is the epitome of all the greed, lust, and general wickedness since the fall of Satan. A minor stereotype is the barmaid. She is immoral by occupation, but she has a heart of gold. She usually helps the good guy at the risk of her own safety. Another minor stereotype is the hero's sidekick. He is usually older than the hero, secondary to him in prowess, and available for the dirty work that the hero can't or won't do. The sidekick also provides what is roughly called "humor," because many times he plays the clown.

Finally, simplified themes are characteristic of most westerns. The themes are often expressed by cliches. The most commonly used seem to be "Cattle rustling doesn't pay," "Good always triumphs over evil," and "Arrogance leads to downfall; humility leads to victory." Also, many of the themes tend to emphasize violence in the solution of problems. For instance, the villain seems to understand only a good physical beating, and the hero can and will beat hell out of the villain because God and Right are on the hero's side.

Thus, the purchase of a new western will likely have nothing to do with "new." In this case of the western, it will mean simply that one bought the latest version of the same old plot, character, and theme.

Danny Fry

Elementary School Personnel

The basic purpose of the work force in an elementary school is to see that the children are well cared for and safe, for only in a secure atmosphere can any real learning take place. Many people in a school help carry out this job: the custodial staff and the lunchroom crew; the school nurse, the teachers and their aides, and the secretary/ and the principal. Each works independently and all work collectively to make the school run safely and efficiently.

The custodial staff is very important in making the school physically safe for the children. Their job is to make sure that the grounds present no dangers to the children. In the buildings, they are in charge of the maintenance of all of the important aspects which directly affect the children, such as the plumbing, the heating, cracked windows, and even something as trivial as a broken pencil sharpener. These people help keep the school sanitary by cleaning all areas that could cause health problems.

The need for a good lunchroom crew is obvious; they prepare nourishing, well-balanced meals for the children. It has been proved that there is a direct relationship between diet and a child's ability to learn, so the lunchroom crew plays an important role in contributing to conditions that stimulate the child's education.

The school nurse is responsible for any medical aid the child may need while at school. Even with conditions in the school at maximum safety, children will be children, and there will always be accidents. The nurse becomes someone a child can turn to for comfort and relief.

The teachers and their aides are very important because of their direct influence on the children. They must make the classroom not only interesting and appealing but also comfortable and safe so that the children can be themselves and have room to grow. The mental and spiritual well-being of the children lies in the hands of the teachers and aides.

One of the most important, but perhaps the most forgotten, persons responsible for the smooth running of an elementary school is the secretary. This position is generally held by a person who can type and file, but more important qualifications are those of patience and understanding. The secretary is the shaft on which the wheel turns. This person carries out and follows through on most of the activities that make a school function. The school can carry on for weeks without a principal, but when the secretary is absent, everything seems to fall apart; materials can't be found, and things just generally pile up. Everyone is affected when that seat is empty.

Last, of course, but not least, is the principal who oversees everything. The principal is the omniscient head of the institution. This person is not only responsible for seeing that supplies are ordered and the teachers are present, but also that discipline is administered. The final threat to unruly children is to be sent to the principal's office. Like a parent to all of the children and some of the teachers, the principal is there for advice and counsel on school or personal matters. There is also the position of mediator, as an objective bystander to skirmishes between teacher and pupil, pupil and pupil, teacher and parent, teacher and teacher, and sometimes even pupil and parent. It is through the principal's management of a close-working crew that the school becomes a healthy influence on children.

Cynthia Packman

The Digital Multimeter

The actual "guts" of a digital multimeter, which is a fairly new and popular piece of test equipment used by electronic technicians, consist of three major stages. These stages, when properly matched, make up a very sophisticated electronic measuring device. The stages consist of the volt-ohm-millimeter (VOM) section, the analog-to-digital (A-to-D) section, and the multiplexing-readout section.

The VOM portion of a digital multimeter is made up of components similar to those of a standard analog meter with a moving needle. The volt and millimeter sections are made up of multiplier and shunting resistors. The ohmmeter section must make use of a constant current source which can usually be built up with the use of a Field-Effect-Transistors (FET's). The old kind of moving needle meter used a battery for its current source in this section. Part of the VOM circuitry also consists of components to match its output correctly to drive the A-to-D converter.

The A-to-D converter is very much like the circuitry that is used in some computers. This section consists of components such as 555 timer I.C.'s (miniature, variable clocks) and operational amplifier (op amp) I.C.'s. Other discrete components, including diodes, capacitors, and transistors, are most likely needed along with the I.C.'s to convert analog voltages to digital frequencies.

The final stage, the multiplexing and readout section, is probably the most complicated as far as electronic components are concerned. Several integrated circuits usually do most of the multiplexing job. In earlier-model digital multimeters, many discrete transistors had to be used to make up this section. The most modern multimeters may have only one large I.C. as a multiplexer. On the more popular meters, the readout display consists of three or four seven-segment light-emitting-diode (L.E.D.) readouts. Older types used what were called Nixie tube readouts. These were "tubes" and not modern "semiconductors." There will usually also be a polarity (+ or -) indicator L.E.D.

From an outside look at the case surrounding the multimeter guts, its face will usually have two, or maybe three, rotary switches and probably several pushbuttons. Two or three jacks for the test leads, used by the technician for measuring, must also have their place on the face of the meter. The only other parts to a digital electronic multimeter will probably be batteries or an AC cord for the power supply.

William C. Stribling

EXERCISE

The following are suggested ideas that, in general, indicate a structure; use one of these or supply your own specific subject and write an essay using analysis by structure:

An organization (political party, social club, committee, student council)

A biological structure (flower, cell, protozoa, lung, pine cone, brain)

A manmade structure (bridge, cabin, desk, clock, automobile distributor, computer)

A geological structure or area

A literary work (poem, short story, movie, television show)

Analysis by Function

A functional analysis informs the reader about how something works. Most functional analyses are organized around two steps: (1) breaking the subject into its intrinsic or basic parts, and (2) explaining how each part functions in relation to the entire operation.

A functional analysis may use a sequence approach for its organization. For example, if your subject is "The Gasoline Engine," you could write about how the engine runs by tracing the sequential order of ignition, spark, combustion, power, and so forth. Here, you would explain each step in sequence as it is involved in the overall function of the subject.

A functional analysis may also explain what a thing does. For instance, you could discuss "The Gasoline Engine" and its function, which is to work as the drive power train for automobiles, trucks, buses, ships, airplanes, generators, pump jacks, and so forth. Thus, you would explain the uses or purposes of the functional subject.

The following essays are examples of analysis by function.

● *Sample Essays*

An Industrial Distributor

An industrial distributor is a person who acts as a salesman, yet he must be knowledgeable of the engineering field. The industrial distributor functions as a salesman in several ways. He can either be a distributor of equipment to one or several industrial companies, or be in charge of purchasing equipment for a company, or even distribute his company's product to the open market.

Being a distributor of equipment to one or several companies places the industrial distributor in a salesman's position. In this position, he goes to the companies and actually sells them a product. In selling his product to a company, he must be able to explain why his product is better for the company. For example, when he tries to sell a drill press to a company, he must be able to explain that because of the special gears which his machine has, it would save the company time during the changing of speeds on the drill press, because the gears are designed to be changed automatically with a certain switch. Therefore, the industrial distributor must know of the engineering design of the machine and its parts.

When the industrial distributor is in charge of purchasing equipment for a company, he must know what is needed, where to get the part, and whether there are other parts on the market that would be more beneficial where it will be used. This is done when he has to replace parts for an older machine or when his company needs new equipment. For example, if a part wears out in an old machine and a new part is needed, the industrial distributor has to know where he can get the part at a reasonable price, and he must know whether there is a newer part which could function better in the old part's place. Another case is that if his company has just come up with a new idea for a machine, the industrial distributor must know where he can get the parts for the machine his company wants to build, and he must know which gears would operate best in the machine. It is in this way that the industrial distributor must be well-versed in the engineering field.

When the industrial distributor works for a company that sells to the open market, he must know the proper way of marketing a product. He should know, most of all, which part of the market would be interested in his product. Since he is mainly involved with an industrial company, his product would more than likely be restricted to industrial firms or hardware stores. For example, if his company sells car ramps, and he is in charge of distributing the ramps, he therefore would try to sell his product to auto-parts stores and service stations. This type of distributing does not require an engineering background, but it involves more knowledge of marketing.

Thus, industrial distributors are not just salesmen with a new title; they are engineering technologists who apply their knowledge in the distribution of goods.

Michael Montalvo

The Spleen

The spleen--an oval, flattened gland-like organ located in the upper part of the abdominal cavity--is the largest of the lymphoid tissues. The spleen has four main functions, one of which is in the fetal life and three of which are in the adult life.

In the fetal life, the spleen has a blood-forming function. Until the ninth month of fetal life, the spleen produces red blood cells and granulocytic white cells. During the ninth month of fetal life, the red bone marrow takes over the formation of red blood cells and granulocytic white cells, while the spleen from then on produces only lymphocytes and monocytes. In certain blood diseases, however, the spleen reverts to its original fetal function forever.

In the human adult, the known functions of the spleen are threefold. As a part of the reticulo-endothelial system, the spleen has the important task of phagocytizing (destroying) the worn out red and white blood cells and blood platelets, as well as the breaking down of hemoglobin into bilirubin and hemosiderin. The spleen is one of the richest iron reservoirs in the body. Second, it acts as a filter for bacteria, protozoa, and foreign particles in the blood stream. Finally, as a lymphoidal organ, the spleen is the chief formative source of circulating lymphocytes, especially in youth and early adult life. As a circulatory organ, the spleen functions as a reservoir of red blood cells from which lymphocytes and red blood cells may be withdrawn in case of an emergency.

Roberta S. Ortiz

The Truck Driver

Most people think that a truck driver is just someone who is too dumb to do anything else. A lot of people think that a truck driver and his vehicle are in the way of all the traffic on the highway. Whatever people think of the truck driver, he is important. The driver, besides being a driver, is also a diplomat and a public servant.

The truck driver as a driver has many things to do before he even starts his run. The only thing that he may know before he starts is his destination. When he arrives at work in the morning or night, depending on when his run starts, he first reports to the shipping office and picks up his dray tickets or manifest. From these dray tickets or manifest, he will find all the information he needs, such as tractor number, trailer number, weight of the load he will be hauling, and his destination. The driver then proceeds to his tractor, checks it out, and, if everything is in working order, he hooks up to the trailer. He then checks the tires and marker lights on the trailer; if they are okay, the truck driver is on the road.

When the truck driver arrives at his destination, the driving part of the job is over, and the diplomatic part of his job begins. Customer relations are very important. The driver finds the receiver or shipping clerk, who will then <u>instruct</u> the driver as to which <u>ramp</u> or <u>dock</u> he wants the trailer spotted. After the trailer has been spotted at the dock, the driver talks awhile to the shipping clerk, for this serves two purposes. It serves to establish customer relations, and, at the same time, the driver learns of the unloading procedures. Usually the customer unloads the trailer, but there are times when the driver has to help. Whichever the case may be, the customer relations will be established. When the customer unloads, the driver will head for the coffee room where he will meet some of the managing personnel. Since the driver is in such direct contact with the customer, his job as a diplomat is very important.

The truck driver is also a public servant. A few years ago, everything was shipped by rail, but this is no longer true. Today, 75 percent of everything is shipped by freight, which is the truck driver and his truck. He hauls merchandise from rail to market, from ship to market, from factory to market, and from factory direct to customers. Industry could not possibly keep up with consumer needs without the truck driver. It sometimes takes weeks to receive merchandise by rail, where it takes only a few days by truck, and in some areas of the market, only one day. The consumer would really be disappointed when he arrived at his favorite market place only to be told there would not be any merchandise for weeks because it was tied up in rail shipment between here and Timbuktu. A truck driver does not tolerate this kind of breakdown. When a truck breaks down, the driver phones the terminal and asks that another truck be brought to the load. The trailer is then hooked up, and the merchandise is back on the road. The truck never stops rolling. In his role as a public servant, the truck driver is very important to the consumer.

The truck driver, in his various roles, deserves a kind word. The motorist, who is also a consumer, should remember that the truck in front of him on the uphill grade is hauling his next purchase at the supermarket or department store.

Charles Tidball

EXERCISE

The following are suggested ideas about which you might write an analysis-by-function essay. You will note that some of these ideas were suggested for an analysis by structure. Make sure your purpose and emphasis is on function rather than on structure. Select one of these or one of your own and write your essay.

- An organization
- A biological structure
- A man-made structure
- A particular job
- A particular institution

Analysis by Process

Process analysis is often called "how to do something" or a "how something was done" exposition. This kind of essay, depending on the purpose of the writer, usually does one of two things: First, it may give instructions to the reader on how to accomplish something, such as how to build a birdhouse, how to make a formal speech, or how to prepare for a vacation to Lake Cuitzeo, Mexico. Second, it may discuss how something was done, such as how the North won the Civil War, how the Rocky Mountains were formed, or how Stonehenge was built.

Many instructors ask their students to avoid the impersonal use of the second-person pronoun *you* (see page 21) when writing an essay of this type. The use of the pronoun *you* to refer to the general reader(s) can be avoided if the writer sets out to describe how something is done rather than to give directions for the accomplishment of the process. The focus in such a description of process is on the activity and the resulting accomplishment rather than on the person accomplishing the process.

If your purpose is to tell the reader how to do something, organize the paper around the parts needed, the implements needed, the conditions necessary, and the steps involved in taking a given number of parts and constructing a finished product. Discuss the steps in a logical order. In other words, make sure that if one step has to be completed before another can be completed, the steps are discussed in a progressive, sequential, order.

If your purpose is to inform the reader about how something was done, describe the steps involved in reaching the final result. Most often, a process essay of this kind is organized around chronological-time order.

The following essays are examples of analysis by process.

● *Sample Essays*

How to Make Orange Brandy

The art of making good orange brandy is very simple, if you follow the basic steps involved. The purpose of this paper is to prepare you, the future wino, to make up to 150 gallons of tax-free brandy in a few simple steps. The process itself is not hard at all. To get started, you need some basic equipment: a ten-gallon crock (a cylindrical, clay-glazed pot), a pizza pan to set on top of the crock, a large cloth to cover the crock and lid, four wine bottles with corks, and a strainer. As far as ingredients, you will need five pounds of sugar, forty-five ounces of raisins, six large oranges, six large lemons, four quarts of boiling water, and one dry yeast packet. There are four simple steps; if followed, you will be rewarded with a good, cheap drunk.

The first step in making orange brandy is normal kitchen technique. Peel the oranges and lemons; as soon as the fruit is peeled, poke them full of holes with a knife. This will help the yeast that is to be added later to make the fruit ferment and convert the fruit juices into alcohol. As soon as this is done, put the fruit into the crock; then add the five pounds of sugar, the forty-five ounces of raisins, and the four quarts of boiling water. Stir the ingredients for about fifteen minutes. This is just to start that wonderful process of nature called fermentation.

After the brew has started to ferment (you should know when it does because it sounds like a vulgar bowl of Rice Krispies), you go back to the sink and fill a measuring cup with cool water. At this point, it is important to know that hot water will kill yeast used in the brandy to speed up the fermentation process. Now if the crock ingredients have cooled to room temperature, then you are ready to add the one cup of dissolved yeast. To make sure that the ingredients are at room temperature, simply place your hand in the solution, and if it feels neither hot nor cold, then it is room temperature. Do not worry about putting a hand in the crock; what the customers do not know cannot hurt them. Besides, any artist knows not to show an unfinished product to a patron. The next step is to cover the crock, first with the pizza pan, then with the cloth. Now put the crock in an out-of-the-way place and let it sit for twenty-five days, stirring daily.

After the brandy has been in the crock for twenty-five days, strain and bottle the brandy. To do this, a strainer and another pot will be needed. There is an important point to know here. Make sure if an aluminum pot is used for a second pot that you do not use it for more than a few minutes because alcohol will oxidize aluminum, which can make the drinker extremely sick. Place the strainer on top of the second pot and empty the crock, taking out all of the large fruit sediment. After straining, put the bottles into the oven and set the dial on "warm." The bottles should be left in the oven for about eight minutes; any longer and the alcohol content might be reduced. Take the bottles out of the oven and cork them. Now put the bottles on a shelf or wine rack, and let them sit for another fifteen days. The longer the bottles sit, the more mellow the brandy becomes.

The next step is the part you have been waiting for--the consumption of the orange brandy. If the proper equipment has been used, the ingredients were the right ones, and the instructions followed, the brandy just made should be very good. I have had two different batches tested by a chemistry major, and the brandy runs from sixty-five to eighty proof, which is actually stronger than normal brandy. But it is legal to make brandy. So open up your first bottle and complete the final step--drink!

Carmault B. Jackson, III

On Becoming a Cowboy

It seems that almost all young adults have to belong to a certain group or type of people. During the early sixties, everyone wanted to be a surfer. After that desire died down, everyone wanted to be a hippie. Now it appears that more and more people want to become cowboys. Actually, becoming a cowboy is a remarkably easy process and can be broken down into three major steps: one must have the proper attire, one must have the proper habits, and one must go to the proper activities.

Probably the most important thing in becoming a cowboy is having the proper dress. First, one has to have boots. The boots should be fairly expensive, because only drugstore cowboys and eastern dudes wear inexpensive, cheaply made boots. Next, one must purchase a hat. It doesn't really matter how expensive the hat is as long as it is western style. Also, in the southwestern states, a straw hat will do just as well as a felt hat, all year around. Third, one will need blue jeans, and just any kind will not do. Jeans must be either Levi or Wrangler brand if a person wants to be a real cowboy. One must also have proper shirts. Prices and brands are unimportant as long as the shirt has a western style, which is characterized by a back yoke and pearl snaps on the sleeves, pockets, and front. Last, one will need a western belt and buckle to round out his cowboy attire. The belt should be handworked with leather stitching along the edges. Also, one's name can be etched in the center of the belt if one desires, expecially if it is a common masculine name such as Buck, Bill, Gene, or Joe. Names such as Diogenes and Archibald are not exactly appropriate, for obvious reasons. The belt buckle should be one of two types: either a gold and silver model depicting a rodeo scene, such as a calf roper or bronc rider in action; or a silver model inlaid with genuine turquoise. After one has acquired the proper attire, he is ready for the second step in becoming a cowboy.

The second step involves the habits or idiosyncrasies one must now adopt. One important habit is cussing. One must lace every sentence with three or four cuss words to maintain the proper image. It is also mandatory that one start chewing tobacco or dipping snuff. This is important because everyone knows that all real cowboys, right down to Walt Garrison, spit tobacco juice. As mandatory as one's chewing habits are one's drinking habits. The only beer that is acceptable is either Pearl or Lone Star; the only hard liquor that is acceptable is either Wild Turkey or Southern Comfort. One must also forget all manners if he wants to be a cowboy. In fact, one must usually be out-and-out rude to people. The best way seems to be to forget about everybody else and think only of oneself. Also, if one is physically big enough, he can push smaller people around and act tough every chance he gets. If one can fulfill these required actions, the rest will come naturally.

The third phase involved in becoming a cowboy is adopting the activities required to complete one's image. There are certain things that a person must do to maintain his status as a cowboy. A major activity is rodeoing. It is not mandatory that one participate, but it is mandatory to show up at the arena at least once a week. If anyone should ever question his authenticity, all he needs to do is ride a bull once. After all, saddle bronc riding requires a saddle and some skill, but anyone can borrow a surcingle and ride a bull for at least one jump. It is also of great importance that one patronize dance halls. The only dance one needs to know is the "Cotton-Eye Joe." Knowing other dance steps will add a bit of flair, but they are really nonessential. One also needs to go to somebody's ranch once or twice a year so that everyone will know about one's ranching experience. One doesn't need to tell that all of this experience involved sitting on the top rail of the horse corral trying to look like the Marlboro Man. Finally, one must get roaring drunk about twice a week, preferably in public. People can then identify the aspirant as a really tough cowboy who fits the image.

As one can plainly see, it is not very difficult to become a modern-day "kicker." All one needs to do is fulfill the requirements of attire, habits, and activities, and very few people will question one's authenticity as a true Texas cowboy. Upon completion of these few simple steps, one will be ready to discredit and damage the old-time cowboy's image and justify what the majority of people already think.

Robert Olive

How to Fill Up

More and more of the everyday commodities used in life are costing people more today than they cost yesterday. As the price of imported oil goes up, so does the price of gasoline. Many gas stations are converting to self-serve stations in an effort to keep prices down. One must know how to fill up at a self-serve in order to take advantage of the savings. Filling a car with gas at a self-serve requires three steps: pulling up to the proper pump, putting the gas in the tank, and paying the attendant.

The first step involved in filling the tank is pulling up to the pump, properly! Where the car is stopped depends on the kind of gas one needs. In newer cars, this is usually unleaded, but, in most cases, one would use either regular or premium. One must, therefore, read the label on the pump. The pump must be on the proper side of the car, depending, of course, on where the gas cap is. Some locations are on the left fender, under the license plate, and on the right fender.

The second step involved in filling the tank is putting the gas in the car. The car's gas cap must be removed and put somewhere so that it will be noticed after filling up. Then the handle or gas nozzle is removed from the pump, and the switch is turned to ON. This action clears the pump of its last reading and prepares it for the next one. The gas nozzle is put into the gas tank and the handle on the nozzle is squeezed. When the proper amount of gas, which varies according to the amount of money available, is put in the car, the nozzle is removed and the switch is turned to OFF. The gas nozzle is put back on the pump, and the gas cap is put back on the tank.

The third and last step is paying the attendant. If filling up is done at night, this usually requires that a person have the exact amount of money shown on the pump because night attendants very rarely have change. Some self-serves that are open at night won't even take major credit cards. While handing the money to the attendant seems simple enough, it can be a tricky procedure in the wind. One must keep his or her hand firmly on the money while passing it through the window or else risk losing it to the wind. With all of this accomplished, the driver can drive away.

While all this sounds very elementary, on many occasions

one can observe a customer fumbling all the way through the procedure. If one follows the above steps, filling up a car at a self-serve can be as easy as one, two, three.

Bart Darling

EXERCISE

The following are suggestions for an analysis-by-process essay:

How to construct something (purple martin house, guitar, formal gown, formal dinner, paper dolls)

How to do something concrete (make a formal speech, organize a club, prepare a campsite, collect butterflies, set up an aquarium, catch a bass)

How to do something abstract (study for an exam, think logically, come to terms with religious views, overcome depression, live life with gusto)

How some historical event happened (how Rutherford B. Hayes became president, how William the Conqueror won the Battle of Hastings, how Harold lost the Battle of Hastings, how a ghost town came to be such)

How a natural thing happened or happens (how it rains, snows, or hails; how the life cycle of a plant or animal occurs; how a typhoon is formed; how a rock crystallizes)

Choose one of these categories or another one that you can think of and write an essay using analysis by process.

Analysis by Classification

In developing an idea through analysis by classification, you group, or categorize, the material to give order to it. In other words, you would take individual things and bring them together or divide them according to one or more characteristics. The most important rule to remember is to classify by applying only one principle at a time. This process ensures that the essay will not be inconsistent or logically weak.

The basic approach to classifying should be formal and objective, so that the conclusions drawn in the classification will be essentially the same conclusions that will be drawn by others who study the issue. For example, the formal classification would be one that groups the high schools of one state into classes on the basis of their enrollment. Thus, if the writer uses the Interscholastic League's designation of of classes B, A, AA, AAA, and AAAA, the results would be the same as anyone else's results concerning the same subject.

The following essays are examples of analysis by classification.

● *Sample Essays*

Hydrocarbons

As one begins a study of the composition of this world, chemistry enters into his studies with much repetition and obvious importance. Chemistry can generally be divided into two broad areas: organic and inorganic. Roughly speaking, organic chemistry involves those substances that contain carbon, and there are many of these substances indeed. A further subdivision, therefore, may be inspected and studied with the purpose of understanding the composition of a substance. One such subdivision is the hydrocarbons--those organic compounds that are the simplest from the standpoint of structure and that contain carbon and hydrogen only. There are four series of hydrocarbons, each classified according to the number of covalent bonds between certain carbon molecules. These are the alkane, alkene, alkyne, and cyclic hydrocarbon series.

The alkane series involves the carbon atoms maintaining single bonds between themselves, such as in a chain. The basic building block of this series is the methane molecule, CH_4. Ethane, C_2H_6, follows methane in this series and introduces the basic pattern of all alkanes; that is, the following molecules, such as propane, butane, and pentane, all differ from the preceding one by the addition of one carbon and two hydrogen atoms. This is known as a homologous series. Examples of familiar alkanes are gasoline, cooking gas, kerosene, and diesel oil.

The next classification of the hydrocarbons would be the alkene series. These molecules incorporate double bonding between one pair of carbon atoms. The simplest alkene, ethylene (C_2H_4), sets the pattern for the remaining members of this series, because again, they each have one carbon and two hydrogen atoms more than the preceding member. Commercial use of alkenes is not extensive, but ethylene, mixed with oxygen, causes green fruits to ripen, and it is used commercially in this manner.

The next group of hydrocarbons, the alkyne series, involves the utilization of a triple bond between a pair of carbon atoms. Once again, this is a homologous series, with the most important member being acetylene (C_2H_2). Acetylene produces an extremely hot flame due to the release of energy when the triple bonds are broken. The bright light of the acetylene welder's torch results from the carbon's being heated to incandescence.

The last and most unlike of the hydrocarbons are the cyclic hydrocarbons, which share the pattern of homologous structure with the alkene series. However, the distinguishing characteristic of these compounds is their ring structure, where the carbon atoms form a circular pattern (unlike the previous groups, in which chains of atoms were present). The simplest cyclic hydrocarbon is cyclopropane, C_3H_6, and one of the best known is benzene, C_6H_6. These compounds have the unique property of being aromatic. Other common cyclic hydrocarbons include styrene, toluene, and naphthalene.

In summation, the myriad of substances that comprise the hydrocarbon group of organic compounds is indeed of great importance to us in terms of lifestyles and even existence. Without the hydrocarbons, basic patterns of life would be greatly changed, but with them, people can use them to their greatest possible advantage.

Douglas Walton

Uses of the Airplane

Man wanted to fly as the bird does for many hundreds of years. Through the ages he watched the bird float freely in the air currents above. Many attempts were made to build a heavier-than-air flying machine that would soar like the birds. Eventually, the gasoline engine was mounted on a set of wings, and within a short time man was flying. On the basis of its function, man has created a flying machine that will serve him in commerce, in warfare, and for pleasure.

Commercially speaking, the airplane is one of the greatest pieces of machinery that man has built. Unlike the truck, the airplane can cover large distances and carry a great deal of cargo in a relatively short period of time. The airplane can avoid large traffic jams and other obstacles that can delay road freight. In contrast to the large ocean freighters, the airplane is at a slight disadvantage. The freighter is capable of carrying several thousand tons of cargo; the airplane can carry at most twenty tons of cargo. However, what the airplane lacks in carrying capacity, it makes up for with speed. Also, in the world of travel, the airplane industry has the greatest advantage. Today's people are generally in a hurry to get from one destination to another, and this improtant fact is what keeps the commercial airplane in such great demand. Thus, in an age of speed and efficiency, the airplane has become the leader in carrying cargo and people.

As an instrument of war, the airplane's development has become vital to the security of almost every nation. Before World War I, the airplane was used mainly as a social observation post. However, throughout the war, the airplane was used in battle more and more. Military strategists discovered the aircraft's ability to carry weapons, and pilots such as Baron von Richtofen and Eddie Rickenbacker were credited with the destruction of many airfields, gun emplacements, and enemy aircraft. As nations fought more wars, the use of aircraft increased. The military forces of today use the airplane for bombing, carrying cargo and troops, reconnoitering, and transporting nonfighting personnel. In sum, from the Sopwith Camel of World War I to modern jet fighters capable of Mach 6 speeds, the airplane has functioned as a vital instrument of war.

156 The Analytical Essay

In recent years, the airplane has slowly gained in popularity as a pleasure craft. During the 1940s and 1950s, most people spent their leisure time driving by car to a particular location. However, during the 1960s and up to the present day, the vast number of people taking flying lessons and the number of small aircraft being sold testify to the airplane's being used for pleasure. Today, aircraft manufacturers such as Cessna, Beechcraft, and Piper are producing planes that the common person can afford and maintain.

Through the airplane's exceptional speed, the freight industry has grown enormously. In the many wars fought during this century, the airplane has proved itself a most effective weapon. The airplane has also provided a great source of pleasure for many people.

Kevin Morrison

Supervisors,
or
"The Good, the Bad, and the Ugly"

Regardless of the type of job one has, he or she usually has some kind of boss. Even people in business for themselves must work in cooperation with someone else. Most people, however, have an immediate supervisor. In the business world, most supervisors will fall into one of three distinct types according to their attitudes about their jobs. These types are employee-centered, production-centered, and self-centered.

The first type, the employee-centered supervisor, is the most agreeable to work for. He tries and usually gets cooperation from each of his employees. This cooperation generally results in a friendly, easy, open atmosphere in the office or place of business. There is less backbiting and more desire to work for a purpose. Most often, happy people make happy workers, if they can work harmoniously. This type of supervisor tries to set a good example, both in his private and professional life. The employee-centered supervisor would never stay on the phone making personal calls while his employees do all of the work. He also makes his people feel an important part of the business team by giving them team-incentive plans instead of concentrating on competition among themselves. He tries to help his employees with their problems, whether professional or personal. If one of his employees has a serious problem at home, the employee is able to tell his supervisor that he's under heavy pressure, and he can expect this type of supervisor to understand. The same is true for on-the-job problems. An employee can always look to this supervisor to recognize his abilities and potential skills and reward them in turn.

The production-centered supervisor, the second type, is not the best to work for, but he is certainly not the worst. He is, unfortunately, one of the gods of efficiency and specialization. He worries about his equipment, his machinery, his typewriters, and anything else that might break down and prevent work from being done. He comes early and stays late, works through lunch, and even comes in on Saturdays or holidays. He also expects everyone else to do the same thing, as if nothing else matters but work. Production is first at any cost, and that is the most important thing to this type of supervisor. Inconvenient hours or compulsory overtime are just part of the game to this person. He forgets human spirit in his belief that people will sell their dignity and job satisfaction for a price.

The third, and perhaps the worst, is the self-centered supervisor. This supervisor is mainly concerned with finding new opportunities to advance himself in his career. He is constantly on the lookout for a chance to win a promotion, which in turn will win prestige from his family, friends, coworkers, and supervisors. His thirst for recognition and power is as insatiable as that of Napoleon. He does not care whom he steps on in his effort to build an empire. This type of supervisor will often increase his staff until the assistants have assistants. This makes him feel important because of the great number of people he is "handling." This supervisor many times has great intelligence and talent, which he uses to undermine his employees and benefit himself. He impresses his supervisors by taking credit for all of the good work and blaming the mistakes on everyone else. The employee working for this type of supervisor can expect to exist in a world of status symbols. The employee can also expect to be very frustrated because he will have little access to the management to air his problems, or to voice his complaints. This supervisor will never ask his employees' opinions of anything, even excluding employees from all decision making. Even if an employee has a new idea, and if it is put into practice, the supervisor takes all credit due the employees.

Most people cannot be pleased all of the time, but jobs are crucial to most people's lives. So, which supervisor would be the best to please and be pleased by--the "good," the "bad," or the "ugly"?

Jacqueline J. Halsell

Acculturation of a Monster

Have you ever noticed how Hollywood has always modernized the Frankenstein monster to fit the times? They do it every time a new Frankenstein appears on the screen, and it goes back as far as 1910. In those first few years of the twentieth century, folks were eager to see love, honor, and justice conquer evil. It was the age of wholesome good sense, at least as far as the infant movie industry was concerned. In the 1910 <u>Frankenstein</u>, the evil monster evaporated in a wisp of smoke when he was confronted with the power of love. With the monster gone, Dr. Frankenstein could marry his girl friend and live happily ever after. But it didn't last long. World War I was just around the corner, so there was a real evil threatening our security. Since it was an age of love and hope, folks didn't want to face the mon-

---

Source: Bob Polunsky, "Flicker Footnotes," *The San Antonio Light: Southwest Today,* August 11, 1974, p. 8. Reprinted by permission of the author and the publisher.

strosity of impending war. Once again, the movies pictured it that way, and, once again, it was with the Frankenstein monster. In the 1915 Life Without a Soul, Dr. Frankenstein conjured up a new monster that symbolized all the world's evil. In the end, though, it just turned out to be a bad dream. That's the way audiences of the time wanted it.

It is significant that no Frankenstein films were made during the 1920s. That was a time of carefree happiness for a lot of folks, while others just drifted from one pleasure to another. It was a shallow age, but, at least, there was no time to dwell on the evil in the world. The 1930s made up for that with three Frankenstein films, each with Boris Karloff as the monster who went berserk. In the first film, he acquired a criminal brain; in the second a bride, who screamed when she saw him, was added; and in the third, he was given a best friend who was just as destructive as the monster was. All three acquisitions said something about the age. In order to get ahead in the world in the 1930s, a man had to have a mind already predisposed to crookedness. It was the only way to get ahead during the Depression. At the same time, the common man of the era felt unloved and undesirable, just as the monster with his screaming bride and social-outcast buddy felt. The bride was played by Elsa Lanchester in Bride of Frankenstein, the buddy by Bela Lugosi in Son of Frankenstein. Lugosi was the hunchbacked Igor, the only character who could control the monster. Basil Rathbone played Dr. Frankenstein's son.

During the 1970s, America has taken the monster back to its bosom and refashioned him to fit the moral climate of our time. In the newest Frankenstein the doctor searches for a brain with lascivious thoughts to plant in his brand-new monster. This brain doesn't necessarily have to come from a criminal nor a crackpot, mind you. It just has to come from a guy with lust on his mind. This new twist in plot says quite a bit about modern-day movies. At least it seems there are a lot of movies nowadays with more stress on sensuality than on good sense.

EXERCISE

The following are suggestions that you might use in writing an analysis-by-classification essay:

Specific people (students, teachers, politicians)

Specific things (governments, institutions, cultures)

Biological things (mammals, reptiles, insects, trees)

Kinds of things (rocks, stamps, sports, movies, languages)

Things according to their function (vehicles, workers, musical instruments, doors)

Select one of these categories or supply one of your own and write your essay.

Analysis by Cause/Effect

Cause/effect analysis is the explanation of the causes or effects of something. You can organize this type of analysis in one of two ways—cause-to-effect or effect-to-cause.

CAUSE-TO-EFFECT ANALYSIS
Using cause-to-effect analysis, you would state a cause and then carefully examine the effects or results that this cause has produced or will produce. For example, you could use as your thesis sentence, "A polluted Edwards Aquifer will hurt San Antonio." The essay would then discuss the effects that this cause would have on the environment, the economic growth, and the people of San Antonio.

The following essays are examples of cause-to-effect analysis.

● *Sample Essays*

The Rh Factor

Every prospective parent has heard about, and most likely feared, the Rh factor in blood types. Many times this fear is well-founded because of the effects that the Rh factor can have on the pregnant mother and the fetus. Specifically, the Rh factor in Rh-negative mothers who carry an Rh-positive fetus has one main effect on the mother and three effects on the fetus.

An Rh-negative mother has no antigen in her blood for the Rh factor. When she becomes pregnant and the fetus has Rh-positive blood, the mother's system begins to form antibodies against the Rh-positive factor of the fetus. The antibody formation is the only effect the Rh factor has on the mother.

The fetus is affected by the Rh factor in three ways: First, the antibodies produced by the mother destroy the fetal red blood cells. Second, because the red blood cells are destroyed, the oxygen supply to the fetal nervous system is also destroyed. Because the fetal nervous system is just developing, it needs a vast amount of oxygen, and the red blood cells carry the oxygen to the fetal nervous system. When the antibodies produced by the mother destroy the fetal red blood cells, they also destroy the oxygen required for fetal development. Third, because of the destruction of the fetal red blood cells, a condition known as "erythroblastasis fetalis" develops. This is the production of immature red blood cells that are still nucleated and unable to carry much oxygen. In an effort to counteract the lack of healthy red blood cells, the fetus makes erythroblasts at a very rapid rate and releases them immaturely. This causes in the fetus and the resultant child such weaknesses as jaundice, anemia, and edema.

Roberta S. Ortiz

Petroleum Boycott

As we all know, the United States is not very independent when it comes to the subject of petroleum. It therefore poses great problems when something goes wrong with our petroleum supply. If the Arabic petroleum countries again boycotted the United States as they did two years ago, there could be a number of adverse effects on the economy of the United States. Three of these effects are price increases of petroleum and petroleum-related products, a shift from purchases of luxury cars to economy cars, and government restrictions and laws.

As the boycott begins, all of the prices start to increase. However, the first big price change that everyone notices will be that at the gasoline pump. Increases of ten to fifteen cents a gallon will be seen. Gasoline is not the only thing that will increase in price. As you will soon notice, almost everything will rise a little bit in price (inflation), if it has any kind of connection at all with the petroleum product. Also, the consumers in the home will be faced with higher electricity bills, depending on which source their electricity comes from. They will be urged to conserve electricity.

This will also result in a big slowdown in the sales of gas-eating luxury cars because prices of gasoline and oil make feeding these monsters expensive. Because of this, most of the car manufacturers are switching their emphasis from the big car to the economy car.

If the pricing does not discourage the consumers, the government might have to intervene and put some sort of gasoline-rationing program into effect. This would consist of handing out gas coupons to all people who are eligible to drive motor vehicles. The government can reduce the speed limit in a further attempt to limit gasoline usage. Gas stations might be asked to close on weekends or after certain hours, in order to discourage drivers from taking long trips during the period of the boycott.

Finally, although a boycott has already been effected against the United States once, if it were to happen again in the near future, we would have about the same results we had two years ago. Those results were inflation and recession.

Greg Maenius

EFFECT-TO-CAUSE ANALYSIS

Using effect-to-cause analysis, you would state an effect or result and then discuss the cause or causes for that effect. For example, you could again take the subject of the Edwards Aquifer and write a thesis that indicates an effect, such as "Why the Edwards Aquifer is Polluted." You would then organize your paper around such causes as industrial waste, poor farming and ranching techniques, poor supervision by state and local authorities, apathy on the part of the people, and so forth.

You should be aware of the logic involved in any causal relationship. If you state emphatically that a result or an effect had a specific cause or causes, you can check your logic by assuming that if the causes are removed, then the effects are also removed. Keeping this logical relationship in mind will prevent you from being too general or emotional in your discussion, thus avoiding a faulty causal relationship.

The following essays are examples of effect-to-cause analysis.

● *Sample Essays*

Man's Traps Threaten the Wolf's Existence

The wolf faces extinction if man does not stop his dangerous methods of controlling these animals. The methods used most often for destroying and regulating wolves today are steel traps, snares, and poison. These are used mainly by government personnel and private citizens motivated by the payment of bounties from public and private sources. All of these techniques are extremely effective on the wolf when they are applied intensively, both because the wolf travels in packs and because the animals live in such sparsely populated areas. When a person wipes out one pack, he may be destroying the whole population in one area from fifty to five thousand square miles. Therefore, if public opinion so dictates, man can now exterminate the wolf from the entire earth within a few years by using the techniques of steel trapping, snaring, and poisoning.

Steel traps are devices that when triggered cause a set of strong jaws to spring around an animal's foot and hold it firmly. The trap is buried shallowly near natural or artificial scent posts, around carcasses of large animals, on wolf trails, or in front of small baited holes known as "dirt holes." Wolf urine and a powerful smelling scent are often used near the trap. Traps are especially effective in autumn when ground conditions are good for setting them. However, they have the disadvantages of being fairly expensive and difficult for the trapper to transport.

The disadvantages of the steel trap can be completely overcome by the use of snares. These devices are made of wire, small cable, or extremely strong rope set in a sliding loop and hung along wolf trails or in other areas where wolves are found. The wolf accidentally sticks its neck into the loop and chokes itself to death. Snares are inexpensive, light, simple to set, and easy to keep operational in cold or snowy weather.

The last method, poisoning, is no doubt the most effective method of controlling wolves. The methods for using poison are the same for all compounds except cyanide, which is fired from a small gun implanted in the ground. This "getter," as the device is known, is triggered when the wolf chews on the baited end sticking up from the ground, and the poison blasts into the wolf's mouth. All of the other poisons are placed in carcasses or in chunks of bait. These latter can be dropped onto frozen lakes from aircraft as well as left by other methods around the wolves' territory.

Man's attempts to regulate these animals have almost succeeded in exterminating them. Factors such as bounties are partly responsible for these killings. But the fact right now is this: The methods of steel trapping, snaring, and poisoning will soon wipe out the wolf if the public does not take action to protect this species against the danger of extinction.

Sara Lee Corkhill

Children with Reading Problems

Teaching reading at an elementary school in Fayetteville, North Carolina, can be a frustrating and bewildering job. It was soon apparent that the reasons those children had reading problems could be traced back to their family situation. The family backgrounds can be grouped in the following way: low income; broken homes; and non-English-speaking.

Low-income families seemed to be typical of the black and Indian people of the area, but there was also a small group of white children who came from this background. All of these children received free breakfasts and lunches from the school every weekday. Their families were large and the children were generally good natured and lovable; also, they were obviously neglected, judging by their grooming habits and manners. The parents of these children were educated through about the tenth grade, and none over the twelfth grade. There were no books, no magazines, no newspapers in the home. Due to this lack of stimulation, the children and no interest or desire to learn to read, and the parents did little to encourage them.

The second classification, children from broken homes, describes nearly as many children as that of the low-income families. Some of these children came from broken homes where the mother may have divorced and remarried as many as four times. A few of the mothers had never even married at all. These unhappy arrangements seemed to be taken out on the children, as many came to school with black eyes and swollen lips. These were generally lower- and lower-middle-class families, and the children seemed uncared for. Many of these children had emotional and therefore behavioral problems. They were moody and often restless and had too much on their minds to be concerned with reading and language arts.

The last group, children with one or two non-English-speaking parents, also had reading problems. Fayetteville is a military city, and so there are a number of military men married to Korean, Vietnamese, German, and Panamanian women who could speak little, if any, English. They certainly could not read any English, and so the children again were deprived of parental support and encouragement. These children's main problem was that they confused words and sounds between the language spoken at home and the language taught at school.

There were, of course, children who did not fall into any of these three categories, and there were some who fit more than one. The greatest percentage of the reading students, though, were apparent victims of their environments.

Cynthia Packman

EXERCISE

The following suggestions lend themselves to writing both types of cause/effect essays. Choose one, making sure your purpose is to examine either the *results* of your topic (cause-to-effect) or the *reasons* for your topic (effect-to-cause), and write your essay.

Poverty
Alcoholism
War
Divorce
Crime
Suicide

SECTION 4

The Persuasive Essay

So far, the examples given in this book have dealt with exposition, that is, the explanation of a topic. However, **argument** is not so much an attempt to explain, although explanation is certainly required, as it is an attempt to persuade a reader to believe your premises and conclusions (or, at least, to sympathize with the issue). Because you should appeal to the reader's intellect instead of to his or her emotions, you should attempt to persuade by using logic.

Logical Argument

A reader may be logically persuaded by the use of **inductive** reasoning (reasoning from specific data from which you draw conclusions) and by **deductive** reasoning (reasoning from a general premise from which you draw specific conclusions). An argument, then, consists of two basic parts, a premise and a conclusion. You should usually state the thesis in such a way that the argument appears therein.

The following essays are examples of logical argument or persuasion.

- *Sample Essays*

Accountability: Why Not For Students?

The Doctrine of Accountability appears to have acquired a status among some urban community colleges approximately equal to that of the Doctrine of Grace among Christians. Among adminis-

---

Source: Lawrence Bell, "Accountability: Why Not For Students?" *TCJCTA Newsletter*, III (November, 1972), p. 5. Reprinted by permission of the author and the publisher.

trators of the larger, more progressive community colleges, there has been a positive "Roueche" to get on the bandwagon. In simplest form, the most essential meaning of Accountability is that everyone is answerable to someone for the quality of the performance of his appointed tasks. Along with the current emphasis on Accountability comes an equally heavy emphasis on Evaluation, for it is but a truism that if there is to be Accountability, there must first be an evaluation of performance.

Members of the Tarrent County Junior College community have certainly been made aware of this emphasis on Evaluation and Accountability and the administration's expressly stated endorsement of the trend. Even now there are committees working hard on devising means to evaluate faculty performance more accurately so that Accountability can be more fully implemented. Accountability for faculty members is clearly <u>de rigueur</u>.

But the most intriguing thing about the current emphasis on Accountability is that it is not applied to students. In fact many classroom instructors are gleaning the distinct impression that to hold students strictly accountable for their academic performance and their personal behavior while on the campus is frowned upon and considered reactionary by many in the vanguard of the community college movement, including some of our own administration. Hopefully, the impression is false and not well grounded; but it is a strong impression and widely shared by the teaching faculty.

Over the past couple of years, even as Accountability was becoming the reigning concept, there has been developing a significant movement toward the avoidance of evaluating students' performance and of assigning grades to it. The pass/fail or credit/no-credit systems have never had more advocates or more friends in court. The deadline for dropping a course without penalty, regardless of performance, has been moved back almost to the final exam. The giving of Incompletes has been liberalized greatly. Teachers are told--often by high-priced visiting consultants--that all student failures are their own personal failures. Students never fail; only teachers do. It is only the rare faculty member who today would dare to correct a student's personal behavior on campus, whether he be using foul language in the mall or engaged in heavy petting in the hallway.

We seem to be trending [sic] toward the curious position of regarding it as reasonable and fair to hold the Board strictly accountable to the public for the overall condition of the district, to hold the administration strictly accountable to the Board for the quality of administration, to hold the faculty strictly accountable to the administration for teaching effectiveness, but to hold the students accountable to no one for much of anything. If Accountability is good for everyone else in higher education, why is it bad for students?

This reluctance to hold students to any very specific or very high standards of performance and behavior is especially odd when considered in the context of our society's recent attempts to recognize students as adults. At age 18 a person is now legally considered mature enough to be drafted or to volunteer for military service, to vote or marry. If he botches any one of these, he has to live with the consequences. Yet on this, and apparently on many other, community college campuses, some administrators and faculty members wish to continue to treat students as children and to excuse them from the consequences of their poor performance or nonperformance.

It is precisely the point of this paper to suggest that Evaluation and Accountability are good ideas and that they should be rigorously applied to students' academic performance and to their personal behavior while on campus. This is more than just a good idea; it is a positive, affirmative _duty_ of any institution of higher education. Whether one likes it or not, we do live in a competitive society in which our students will be evaluated by and held accountable to several different masters: employers, different governments, mates, and peer groups of various types. We are not preparing them to live in this society by lowering our standards or excusing them from the consequences of poor performance. In the long run, we do them a definite disservice by letting them off easy.

Experience teaches us that failure in some things is a part of life. Psychologists teach us that learning to tolerate a certain amount of failure and to react constructively to it is essential to the development of good mental and emotional health. Moreover, the very essence of maturity or adulthood is making one's own decisions, accepting the consequences of one's actions, and boldly standing responsible for them. Are these the attitudes we are fostering by the current trends toward relaxation of the standards for academic performance and personal behavior? Clearly, we are not.

It is a fair question to ask, "Well, what exactly would you have us _do_ here and now?" First, we who teach at Tarrant County should _raise_ our academic standards, not lower them. This is most needed in regard to the awarding of A's and B's, which are in danger of becoming meaningless in some areas due to the ease by which they are obtained. We also need to admit without embarrassment that some students, despite our very best efforts, simply will not put forth sufficient effort to earn passing grades. As adults, these students must accept the consequence of their lack of effort. We teachers must quit kow-towing to the myth that an F or WF is a punitive grade vindictively assigned by a malicious teacher. It is rather a symbol awarded as a result of a professional judgment that a given student has not performed a specific responsibility at even a minimally acceptable level. If a teacher does not have enough professional self-confidence to make that judgment, he is in the wrong profession. So long as the task and its objectives have been made clear along with the methods and criteria of evaluation, the teacher has an affirmative duty to make his evaluation and to render a professional judgment. And the student must accept the consequences of his performance. *That* is accountability!

Secondly, the administration must not become inordinately concerned that a teacher may have awarded a significant number of D's, F's, W's, and WF's unless that number is consistently and unreasonably high. What is reasonable? Undoubtedly it varies among courses and programs. In the social sciences some take it as a rule of thumb that an effective teacher usually ought to be able to get 70% of his students to complete the course with a grade of C or better, based on the total twelfth-day student load. Above all we must reject the in-vogue canard that "students never fail; only teachers do." Any classroom teacher encounters some students who seem almost hell-bent and determined to flunk; and some refuse to be salvaged. If students have a right to be treated as adults, then they have the responsibility to perform acceptably or to be adjudged failures.

Thirdly, if regular attendance at a formal class and/or the completion of a term-paper and/or outside projects or packaged instructional units are required for completion of a course, and if this is made clear at the outset of the course, then the instructor should rigorously and equitably enforce these requirements. The students must be evaluated and judged on their performance. That is not only Accountability, but from the viewpoint of the other students it is also Equal Protection under the Law!

Finally, in regard to *any* of our school policies affecting student behavior on campus, as long as those policies remain in effect and are clearly stated for all to see, we should not be embarrassed or reluctant to enforce them. Constant reexamination of our policies may well be advisable; but as long as our policies are clearly stated, enforcement of them is merely the application of the Doctrine of Accountability.

Lest any should misconstrue the intent here, nothing in this paper is intended to derogate or call into question our open-door policy, remedial instruction for those who need it, special consideration for the handicapped, genuine faculty concern for students' welfare, or the general idea of "going the second mile." What is intended is to say that the Doctrine of Accountability and its Evaluation Corollary are valid. They are valid as applied to the Board, to the Administration, to the Faculty, and to our Staff. Why should they be considered less valid when applied to our students?

Lawrence Bell

Agriculture: A Solution to the Energy Crisis

Dean Fred Benson of the College of Engineering at Texas A & M University predicted that a fuel shortage would occur in the late 1960s and the early 1970s. His prediction caused scientists to experiment with methods by which to solve the shortage. The availability, potential, and cost of the method determine whether it is a solution or not. Agriculture--the science of cultivating the soil or raising livestock--is being tested as a possible solution to the fuel shortage. Because availability, potential, and cost are advantageous as a solution, American agriculture is one of the best solutions to the American energy crisis.

As far as the availability of land is concerned, the United States is sufficiently equipped, with more than 200 million acres of uncultivated land suitable for growing crops. In addition to the abundance of uncultivated land available, an abundance of plants also exists. Plants consist of cellulose, which, when decomposed for millions of years, produce coal, which is then used as fuel. The South is already a major forest cellulose producer with the advantages of ample rainfall and much solar energy.

However, does agriculture have the potential to produce enough fuel to call it a solution? First, a technique known as bioconversion must be considered. It involves harvesting the food parts of a plant and then obtaining energy from the conversion of the plant's wastes, such as stalks and husks, into fuel. Ab Flowers of the American Gas Association says bioconversion of plants or crops and their residues "could potentially produce about ten trillion cubic feet of gas per year." Second, crop residues exist in an abundant quantity. Farno L. Green, a General Motors executive engineer, stated that "agriculture residues left in the fields by United States farmers each year in the forms of stalks, leaves, and husks amount to almost one-half of the heating value of the coal produced in the United States annually." General Motors has already performed experiments in its Michigan plant by mixing 10% cornstalks with 20% coal for boiler fuel. Results then indicated that it would even be possible to mix up to 60% cornstalks with 40% coal and obtain the same potential. Therefore, because the technique of bioconversion has the capacity it does and enough residues do exist, agriculture is a viable solution to the present energy crisis.

However, the cost of this solution is very important to the United States economy. The amount of money spent today on petroleum imports would decrease because of the production of ethylene gas. Researchers at Texas Tech University have taken 180 pounds of ethylene gas from a ton of feedlot manure. Since the plastics industry requires the use of petroleum, ethylene gas can reduce petroleum imports. Texas Tech researcher James Holligan states: "Assuming a realistic value of ten cents per pound for ethylene, estimated value of ethlyene from manure from a 20,000-head feedlot would be about $360,000 per year. The process appears economically feasible for areas of large feedlot concentration." To build more nuclear energy plants, to drill new oil and gas wells, and to develop new shale coal processes by 1980, 500 billion dollars would have to be spent. Since agriculture is a recent solution, marketing for residues will start at a low cost. Collecting and transporting are achieved today by harvesting equipment especially constructed for the collection of residues.

As long as plant life and animal life exist, agricultural residues will also continue to exist. According to Green's calculations, 427 million tons of agricultural residues are produced each year. Therefore, year by year, enormous quantities of residues might eventually have the potential to satisfy over half of our total energy requirements for the future.

BIBLIOGRAPHY

Freeman, S. David. *Energy: The New Era*. New York: Walker and Company, 1974.

Scruggs, C. G. "Can Agriculture Provide an Answer to U.S. Energy Crisis?" *Progressive Farmer* (November, 1975), pp. 244, 266-67.

Joanna Rosas

Illogical Argument

Our discussion of illogical argument will deal with the two basic types of illogical persuasion—propaganda and fallacious argument. Both generally employ specious reasoning; that is, the conclusions do not logically follow the premises, or the causes the effects.

PROPAGANDA

Although the word *propaganda* means the systematic propagation of a doctrine and its views, this denotative explanation of the word accurately reflects neither the modern use of, nor people's attitudes about, propaganda. Since World War II, propaganda has taken on the added meaning of furthering a cause or view or damaging an opposing cause or view. Most often, propaganda, in its attempt to persuade or dissuade, appeals to people's emotions rather than to their intelligence.

For our purposes, we will define **propaganda** as a deliberate appeal to the emotions, prejudices, or preconceived feelings and beliefs of readers. Sometimes a persuasive essay may *appear* to be based on logic when it is actually based on fallacious reasoning; thus, a writer is propagandizing an issue rather than arguing the issue logically.

As a writer and as a reader, you should be aware of several propaganda techniques:

> **Glittering Generalities**—words that have favorable or unfavorable connotations without justifying the use of the terms

Transfer—attaching a favorably connotative symbol to an unrelated issue

Testimonial—attributing testimony or counter-testimony to a product or issue which the person testifying is not qualified to pass judgment on

Plain Folks—appealing to the average person's habits and values in a patronizing manner

Band Wagon—appealing to people's desire to belong to a group

Sex Appeal—playing on people's vanity or gender

Card Stacking—using a combination of the above devices in order to win support by deception, thus stacking the evidence unfairly

The following essay is an example of propaganda.

● *Sample Essay*
___

Oppression in America

Smokers of America, unite! If we don't, sooner or later, the antismoking, puritanical moralists will have us hiding out behind the barn or in the cellar catching a few quick puffs of grapevine or cedar bark. The great American concepts of freedom of choice, free enterprise, and rule by majority are being usurped by a small antismoking minority and their legislative henchmen.

America has flourished and prospered by the idea that what any individual does is strictly that person's own business, unless it hurts someone else. I do realize that a few isolated individuals are adversely affected physically by tobacco smoke, and I will be the first to quit smoking in their presence if neither of us, because of circumstances, has a choice about being together. These people have rights, and I respect them. On the other hand, the majority of antismokers object to smoking because of bigoted, dogmatic, pious, childish, "goody two shoes" principles. These pseudo-moralists aggravate the vast majority of "grass roots" people who do smoke. After all, my physical business is my business, and my moral business is my business, too. Personally,

I'm not going to let officious, nosy snoops who don't have anything better to do control my life. Let them take care of their own souls, and I will take care of mine. So, freedom of choice works two ways, except in the case of tyrannous antismokers. It is my personal choice to smoke, so why do I have to sit in the back of the plane or the bus like some second-rate outcast? The smoker's position today is similar to the black people's plight before civil rights laws did away with discrimination. Since the bigoted rednecks can't make people feel inferior anymore because of their skin color, they have latched onto smokers as their victims. We smokers need a Martin Luther King, a great American, to lead us against the enemy. By the way, why don't these holier-than-thou antismokers sit in the back of the plane and let smokers sit up front? After all, we are good people, too.

Legislatures have already designated by law <u>where</u>, and to some extent, <u>when</u> we can smoke. If we don't watch it, soon there will be tyrannical legislation that we cannot smoke at all. This reeks of totalitarianism and communism, not democracy. Maybe the antismoking hypocrites should design a new national flag which has stitched into the stars and stripes all of the "don'ts," such as "don't smoke." The paranoid antismokers might be able to ramrod adoption of such a flag through a spineless legislature. I personally fought in Korea and Vietnam so that this country could remain free. I won several decorations, including two Purple Hearts, and I was always proud of my role as an American Marine. Nevertheless, I am thinking of sending my decorations to the antismoking organizations. They should know what to do with them. I'm keeping my Purple Hearts, though. I was physically wounded in defense of this great country, and the scars are real. But these wounds in no way hurt as badly as the psychological wounds I have received from the "shots" that the antismoking, un-American element in my own country has directed toward me.

This country was also founded on free enterprise, and the

antismoking element would take that freedom away. Where would America be if all of a sudden tobacco were illegal, as some misguided people advocate? From the small, independent tobacco farmer, to the makers of tobacco products, to the retail outlets and vending companies--doing away with these legitimate businesses would have a drastic, negative effect on our country's economy, perhaps even causing another depression. Do we need the hardworking people in the tobacco industry reduced to begging handouts and subsidies from a welfare agency? The answer to that is obvious to any right-thinking American who values the economic strength of this country.

So why are we, the majority who smoke, letting a minority tell us what to do? We could be gutless and apathetic, but most probably we are too tolerant and kind. We respect the rights of others, and we expect good citizens to respect our own rights. When people criticize us for smoking, they are directly putting down some great Americans: Presidents Eisenhower, Kennedy, and Johnson smoked; great statesmen such as Churchill and Generals Patton and MacArthur smoked.

Just who is this minority? They are mostly little old ladies in tennis shoes who don't have anything better to do. These bluenoses with their air of superiority have cohorts in young, lamebrained women who don't know anything about the real world, and their male counterparts, the Casper Milquetoast weaklings who follow along and mouth the shallow slogans of these domineering women. So why should the real men of the world and all of the free-thinking women stand by and let our freedoms be taken away? Are we men or mice? I think that we have said, "Pass the cheese" long enough to the despotic, antismoking bigots in this country. Come up out of the dark cellars of oppression. Stand up and be counted! Remember, "The only thing we have to fear is fear itself."

Mariposo Dalmane

FALLACIOUS ARGUMENT

A fallacious argument is either deliberate or inadvertent. In either case, it is an error that invalidates an argument. You should take care to understand the logical methods of persuasion, lest you fall into "logical fallacy," either as a writer or as a reader. **Logical fallacy** may use one or more of the following techniques:

Red Herring—begging the question, ignoring the context of the argument, or bringing in a false issue

Argumentum ad Hominem—attacking the man rather than the issue

Hasty Generalization—jumping to a conclusion without evidence

Black-White or Either-Or Fallacy—stereotyping, drawing faulty or inadequate causal relations, or considering only two alternatives when others may be available

False Analogy—forming comparisons between two or more things that should not be logically compared.

The following essay is an example of fallacious argument.

● *Sample Essay*

Obscenity in the Mail

One of the most serious problems confronting the American people is the great tide of pornography that engulfs the nation. Open sewers of filth flow unabated throughout our land. This massive attack on religious and moral standards has a critical impact on our young people.

In my judgment, the growth of obscene and pornographic material is closely related to many other of our crucial problems. When our youth have been taught that our moral, religious, and ethical standards are to be totally disregarded in the area of pornography, then we certainly should not be surprised that a minority of them engage in such acts as burning draft cards and American flags, using heroin and other narcotics, and committing violent attacks on the person and property of others.

Moral and spiritual chaos inevitably results in social and political chaos, which is, of course, the primary objective of communists and other revolutionaries. It is no accident that some leaders of the New Left and other political radicals publicly use obscenity and employ pornography at every opportunity.

In short, this flood of pornography poses a real threat to our social and political structure.

This horrible situation is caused largely by judges, who, for various reasons, decide that the rights of smut peddlers should always be superior to those of the American people.

Recently, the House of Representatives passed a bill that would prohibit the mailing of obscene material to minors and would provide mail patrons with a means not to receive unsolicited, potentially obscene material.

Most of the opponents of efforts to ban obscenity from the mail contend that pornography does not harm children. We know better.

An article in the <u>Reader's Digest</u>, entitled "What Sex Offenders Say About Pornography," tells of personal interviews with more than seventy offenders in Wisconsin and California. About half of the offenders interviewed stated that the availability of pornographic materials was directly related to their commission of sex crimes.

Obscenity should be banned from the mail because it is tearing down the moral, religious, and ethical standards of this country. Pornography poses a real threat to us and should be stopped while there is still time to act.

Name Withheld

EXERCISES

A. Argue a current topic about which people naturally get emotional. Deliberately use as many propagandistic and fallacious argumentative techniques as possible. When you have completed your argument, list the propaganda devices and the kinds of fallacious argument that you used. The following is a list of some topics that might be used; use one of them or another that you choose yourself.

Abortion

Prayer in public schools

Legalized prostitution
Legalized use of marijuana
Student evaluation of instructors
Pornography
Busing

B. Take the subject for your deliberately propagandistic argument and argue one side of the issue in a logically argumentative essay. Attempt to appeal to your reader's intelligence rather than to his or her emotions.